The Art
of Pantomime

The Art of Pantomime

Charles Aubert

Translated from the French by
EDITH SEARS

DOVER PUBLICATIONS, INC.
Mineola, New York

Bibliographical Note

This Dover edition, first published in 2003, is an unabridged reprint of the April 1931 printing of the work first published by Henry Holt and Company, New York, in 1927.

Library of Congress Cataloging-in-Publication Data

Aubert, Charles, 1851–
  [Art mimique. English]
  The art of pantomime / Charles Aubert ; translated from the French by Edith Sears.
    p. cm.
  ISBN 0-486-42857-5(pbk.)
    1. Pantomime. I. Sears, Edith. II. Title.

PN1985.A83 2003
792.3—dc21

2003041459

Manufactured in the United States of America
Dover Publications, Inc., 31 East 2nd Street, Mineola, N.Y. 11501

DEDICATED
TO THE PEOPLE OF THE THEATRE,
ACTORS, SINGERS, DANCERS, PANTOMIMISTS,
AND TO ALL WRITERS, ARTISTS,
PAINTERS, DESIGNERS, SCULPTORS,
ETC., ETC.

CONTENTS

CHAPTER   PAGE

       GENERAL IDEAS 3

       EXERCISES FOR SUPPLENESS 9

       ANALYSIS IN DETAIL OF MOVEMENTS OF THE BODY
             AND ITS MEMBERS 13

       DETAILED ANALYSIS OF THE MUSCLES OF THE FACE . 58

       ANALYSIS IN DETAIL OF MOVEMENTS OF THE HANDS . 78

       COMPLETE REGISTRATION OF EXPRESSION 95

       EXPRESSIONS OF THE ENTIRE HEAD 97

       PASSIVE EXPRESSIONS 123

     I. PANTOMIME IN THE THEATRE 150

    II. HOW TO REGISTER THE PARTS OF SPEECH 155

   III. PROBLEMS OF THE SILENT DRAMA 168

    IV. THE CHOICE OF A SUBJECT 174

     V. HOW TO WRITE A PANTOMIME 180

    VI. HOW TO TRANSLATE IT 185

  VII. THE USE OF THEATRICAL ACCESSORIES 188

VIII. STAGING THE PANTOMIME 194

    IX. THE ACCOMPANIMENT OF MUSIC 202

     X. THE BALLET 209

INTRODUCTION

Pantomime, one of the oldest arts of the theater, has received little attention in our country until very recent years. The term has been applied to such various forms of drama in the long history of the theater that we may well ask what is the real meaning of *The Art of Pantomime.*

In ancient Greece, the pantomime was the actor and also his performance when he translated into gesture or movement the thought which the chorus was expressing. In the rich period of Elizabethan drama the " groundlings " continued to demand the " inexplicable dumb shows and noise " which the farcical pantomimes of the day presented. France, borrowing from Italy and developing the form to a higher degree, made of the *commedia dell' arte* one of the most distinct dramatic forms. Its characters were Pierrot, Columbine, Harlequin; its costumes were formalized, fantastic; its action was limited to certain elements of farce. Molière knew the value of its excellencies and made use of them. To-day in England, the Christmas pantomime is a medley of burlesque, musical comedy, and vaudeville which has forgotten that the term means only the wordless expression of sentiments, emotions, ideas by gesture or movement.

In America we know pantomime chiefly as an element of the interpretative dance. Only rarely has the form been dignified by presentation in the legitimate theater, as in the exquisite interlude of *The Beggar on Horseback* or in the charming pantomime played by Laurette Taylor, *Pierrot the Prodigal.* This kind of pantomime is accompanied and interpreted by music, or it may be itself an interpretation of the music. To-day the most advanced schools in the dance make pantomime an element in training for that art. In fact, it was Miss Elizabeth Gardiner, of the Tchernikoff-Gardiner Studios in Washington, who first brought this treatise of Aubert to our attention. All who are interested in this method of dramatic expression will find *The Art of Pantomime* a valuable contribution.

But the service which this book renders to the technique of the drama is far wider than its application to pantomime proper. Before the moving picture was developed, Charles Aubert had recorded and discussed these innumerable gestures and expressions by which the actor may convey to the eye an idea or an emotion. The moving picture screen may gain much from this treatise with its lavish and illuminating diagrams.

For the legitimate stage too there is material here which offers an opportunity to overcome the limitations and the slackening which many bemoan in the acting of our day. The director who deals with amateur and novice American actors is constantly appalled by the lack of expressiveness in our native face. The "wooden" or "frozen" expression with which our young American expresses the most passionate sentiments has defied many a veteran director. Here is a textbook which should melt the most rigid features into flexibility and expressiveness. As Monsieur Aubert says, " The best way to perfect dramatic work is to play pantomimes," and his diagrams offer to any earnest student of the art of acting a vast variety of opportunities to cultivate and perfect this art.

Those of us who have used the volume in the original French are grateful to Mrs. Sears for putting it within reach of all students and teachers of acting through her faithful translation. We particularly commend to the amateur the chapter on the *Staging of Pantomime*, with its admirable advice to directors, and the many diagrams illustrating facial expression.

SIBYL BAKER
Director, Community Center Department
Public Schools of the District of Columbia

WASHINGTON, D. C.
February 1, 1927

THE ART
OF PANTOMIME

GENERAL IDEAS

The language of action, or dumbshow, is universal; the ways of expressing emotion are identical among different races of mankind.

Pantomimes are theatrical performances played in the language of action.

Acting is the art of registering, by all possible means, but principally by one's self, with one's own body, all the visible movements by which human emotions and thoughts are manifested. The Art of Pantomime is the necessary assistant to any art which attempts to represent man as thinking, feeling or doing.

Above all, the art of expression is the fundamental element of the theater, action being the clearest, the most impressive and, may one say, the most contagious language because the spectator who sees a more or less intense emotion portrayed by acting, finds himself drawn by the power of the quality of imitation, to share and to feel himself the emotion of which all the signs are shown to him.

Indeed, it may be argued that as the object of spoken words in a play is only to explain the motives of action, they should be considered the secondary element, but the contrary is the prevalent opinion. Literature as a means of expression has attained such a high degree of perfection, and, at the same time, action has been so neglected, that it is the latter which passes unnoticed, and the importance of its rôle is not suspected. But the place accorded it signifies little. It offers the benefits of its powerful aid to artists in general, and actors in particular. So it is for them this volume is principally intended.

Acting includes attitudes, facial expressions, and gestures; in fact all bodily movements: it includes also laughter, tears, cries and all spontaneous inflexions of the voice.

Dramatic movements are divided into five kinds, namely:

1. Action movements, which are simply and solely those necessary to perform an act: — to dance, walk, etc.

2. Character movements: — These are permanent, and determine the character, the habits, and the quality of an impersonation.

3. Instinctive movements: — These are spontaneous, involuntary and betray an emotion, a moral or physical sensation.

4. Descriptive or speaking movements: — These are voluntary, studied, constructed and aim to express a thought, a need, a wish; or to describe a person or an object; or to indicate a place or direction.

5. Complementary movements: — These consist of the cooperation of the whole body in the meaning indicated by the chief movement so that this expression is given more force and harmony.

A dramatic expression to be complete requires at the same time: posture, facial expression and gesture. Characterizations consist mostly of postures. Portrayal of emotion is produced mainly by facial expression. Descriptive or speaking action consists mainly of gestures made with the hands.

For an actor, the art of registering consists in gaining:

1. Flexibility and mobility of the body, limbs and facial muscles.

2. Knowledge of all the movements he can execute.

3. Ease and precision in executing these movements.

4. Perfect understanding of the meaning of each of them.

A survey of all the movements which can be executed by the body, the limbs, the muscles of the face, and the hands, will first be taken, and the meaning of each movement noted in passing.

Moreover, just as a person understands better and uses more aptly a word whose etymology he knows, it is true that the import of a movement can be better grasped and carried out with greater exactness if he knows the origin of this movement and its primitive meaning.

We will try to untangle the etymology of gestures, or rather, we will humbly submit some ideas on this subject, though many noted scholars have already treated this subject without coming to an agreement.

In the present line of research, the reader should let himself be guided by the principle of utility. Perhaps in the majority of cases the physiological utility which existed in a primitive state, persists yet, and always will. Really there is no reason why the signs of the desire to weep, (Fig. 1), should not be ex-

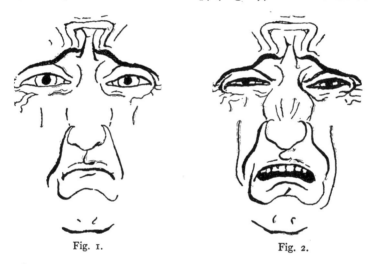

Fig. 1.   Fig. 2.

actly the same among our contemporaries as among our remotest ancestors.

As has been pointed out, all dramatic movements are not of the same nature.

Thus there is a noticeable difference between the instinctive expression of weeping (Fig. 2), where it is evident that all the muscular changes of the face which coöperate to form it occur spontaneously, without control by the will and even against the will, and the speaking expression of imploring, of pitying, where the will is manifest (Fig. 3). Here the expression is at the same time voluntary, studied, and constructed. The lines of the forehead in opposite directions, the brows both raised and drawn together, the cheeks raised and puffed under the eyes, the lips pouting, are indeed the beginning of the act of weeping.

The idea is: I suffer enough to weep. Have pity.

On the other hand, lips which are put forward as if for a kiss, supreme sign of good will, suggest the idea of good: Be good. Give me.

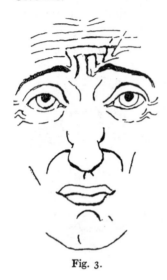

Fig. 3.

Lastly the bent head means: I bow down. I humble myself.

These are not of necessity shown in the face of the beggar. He can take them up voluntarily with the object of exciting pity; they are like a mask which can be removed and put on. In short, it is a language carefully thought out.

To sum up, instinctive movements of expression, which spontaneously take place with the object, doubtless efficacious, of relief, of defense or preservation of the human race, have never varied, they always have the same use, and therefore require no other explanation.

It is not necessary to know *why* grief or physical pain, by action on a certain nerve, forces a certain muscle to move, which in its turn acts upon a certain gland and determines finally a certain grimace at the same time that tears burst forth. These are physiological problems, and their solution is not indispensable to the result sought here.

On the other hand, it is very interesting to analyse speaking expressions, which are usually complex, and which may have had a primitive significance different from the one attached to them today.

It is worthy of notice that instinctive expressions appeal directly and instantly, while often speaking movements are more suggestive, that is, they do not explicitly designate the thing indicated, but suggest it by means of the association of ideas.

Notice carefully the following remarks which readers will have many chances of verifying by pursuing this study:

All expressions which are stamped by will and intelligence, in whatever degree, such as covetousness, anxiety, reflexion, intel. lectual effort, scorn, disgust, horror, anger, defiance, combativeness, bravery, pride, struggle against trouble, etc., are always characterized by drawing the eyebrows down and together, forming at the base of the forehead vertical wrinkles, and are also accompanied by a tension of the limbs and whole body.

Expressions where intelligence and will are inactive for the moment, such as hesitation, ignorance, admiration, stupefaction, fear, extreme physical suffering, gayety, laughter, enjoyment and petulance are always characterized by extreme elevation of the eyebrows which causes horizontal lines on the forehead. They are also accompanied by relaxation of the muscles and flexion of the limbs.

Some of these emotions may be experienced, those for instance against which it would be useful to react, such as anxiety, fear, physical suffering — while still retaining, to a certain point, the will to struggle. In this case cross lines are formed on the forehead; that is, the vertical lines persist in spite of the predominance of horizontal lines. But when these emotions, gaining greater intensity, entirely paralyse intelligence and will, the vertical lines completely disappear.

All the expressions which indicate a resolve, an activity or a charm, such as: to admire, desire, pray, persuade, order, threaten, brave, etc., require that the weight of the whole body be carried on the forward leg, and the head held erect.

On the contrary, all expressions which portray indecision, timidity or dislike, such as to hesitate, doubt, meditate, be frightened, scorn, dread, etc., are completed by throwing the weight of the body onto the backward leg. All expressions of intense emotion impel the raising of the shoulders.

Actors will easily understand that if they leave to actual

pantomimists most of the voluntary or studied expressions whose purpose is to take the place of words, they have, on the other hand, the greatest interest in studying and making use of all instinctive expressions which powerfully contribute vitality to speech by adding to it more light, force and warmth.

It may be emphatically remarked that, apart from a few indicative and descriptive signs, dramatic movements express only verbs, nothing but verbs.

EXERCISES FOR SUPPLENESS

In the language of action, every part of the body should be controlled.

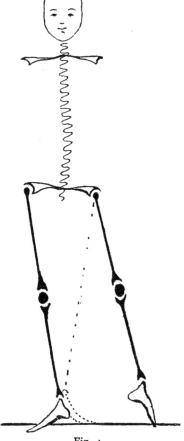

Fig. 4.

It is not enough to make gestures and grimaces. For the registration of an emotion to be complete, the body and all its members must coöperate. The grace, definiteness and power of an actor depend on the harmonious participation of the whole organism. Therefore a comedian should be supple, agile, and graceful. Besides, he must be sure of his balance for, as will

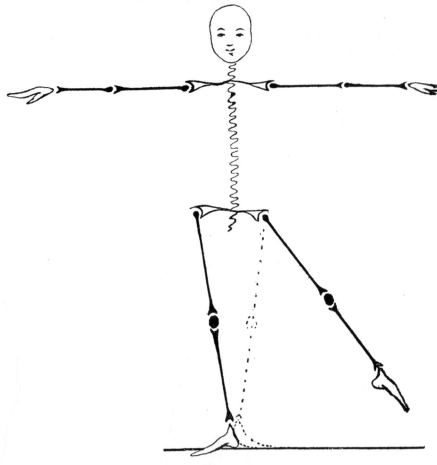

Fig. 5.

be shown later, most postures, to have their full force of expression, demand that the weight of the body rest on a single leg.

The best means of acquiring these qualities is to study the first dance exercises, namely:

Raising the feet from the ground (Fig. 4).

Raising the feet half way (Fig. 5).
Making circles with the legs (Fig. 6).
Bending in five positions (Fig 7).

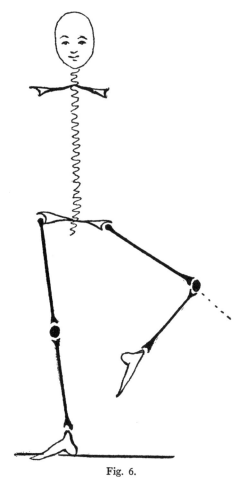

Fig. 6.

These exercises carried out for some time in a regular manner, and occasionally added to, will give the artist precious
qualities which he will always retain.

It is not a question of actually learning to dance, though this
would be no detriment, but only of gaining poise, control and

harmony of movement.   A dancing master will teach these exercises in a few lessons, so no attempt is made to describe them. They are pointed out and definitely recommended.

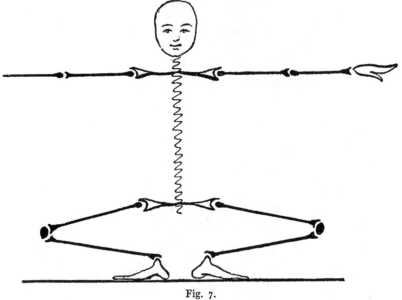

Fig. 7.

During the first days these exercises will cause some soreness in the muscles, but this slight discomfort will soon disappear, while the advantages which will result from such efforts will remain.

ANALYSIS IN DETAIL OF MOVEMENTS OF THE BODY AND ITS MEMBERS

The Legs

To stand erect, legs straight, heels together, with the body supported equally on both legs (Fig. 8), is the posture appropriate to the following sentiments:

Modesty.
Timidity.
Humility.
Respect.
Passiveness.
Servility.
Respectful waiting.

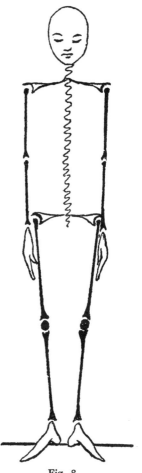

Fig. 8.

To stand, the body resting equally on both legs, but the feet separated (Fig. 9), gives the impression:

Of a sailor.   Of a cavalryman.

Of vulgarity.   Of a blockhead.

Of a man accustomed to carry heavy burdens.

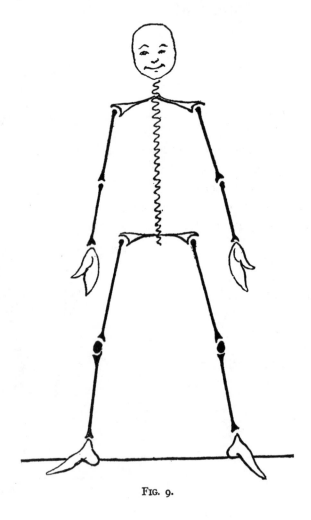

Fig. 9.

Same position as the preceding, with legs bent (Fig. 10), indicates:

Fatigue.   Weakness.   Old Age.   Drunkenness.
In general, the fear of losing one's balance.

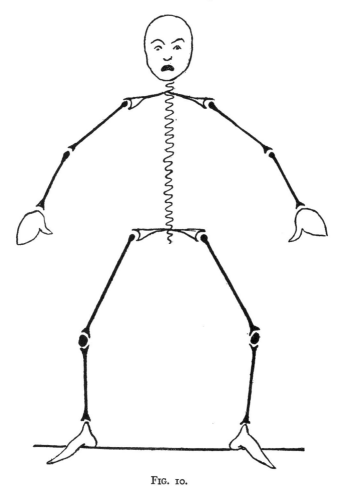

FIG. 10.

To stand erect, facing the audience, both feet on the floor, but the body's weight sustained by one leg only, produces more graceful, active and expressive postures.

If the body rests on the leg opposite the action that is taking place (Fig. 11), an attitude of indifferent waiting results.

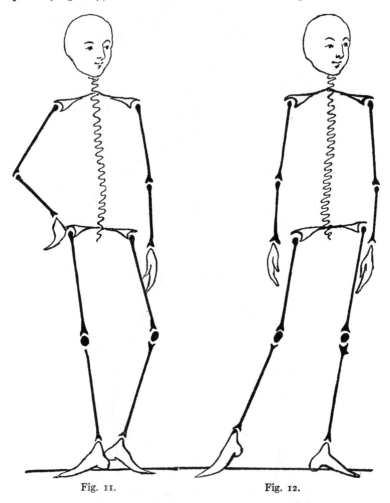

Fig. 11.   Fig. 12.

If the hand rests on the hip, it must be the right one, when the body rests on the right leg.

If, on the contrary, the body is supported by the leg on the side towards the action (Fig. 12), the attitude is:

Active.   Attentive.

When addressing an audience or a partner, if the body rests equally on both feet placed on a line (see Figs. 8 and 9) the least expressive and least easy position results, as the body can-

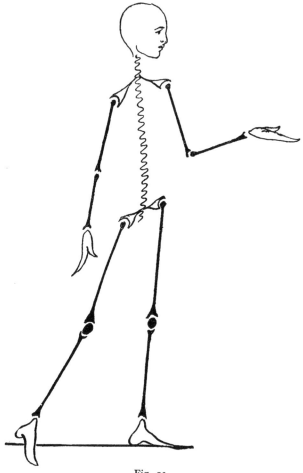

Fig. 13.

not be moved forward or backward without danger of losing its balance.

On the other hand, if one foot is forward (Fig. 13), you can give to the body forward or backward movements which will result in postures of powerful effect.

The attitude of carrying the body on the forward leg conveys the following emotions:

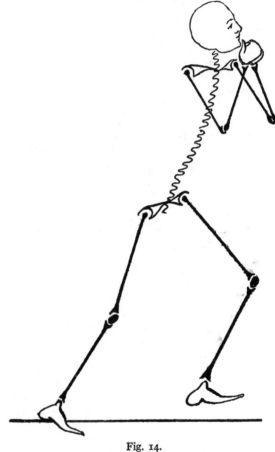

Fig. 14.

To struggle.	To admire.	To supplicate.	To promise.
To order.	To desire.	To wish.	To observe.
To threaten.	To ask.	To affirm.	To persuade.

In general, all expressions controlled by will.

Bending the leg which supports the body gives the same expressions (Fig. 14), but much more accentuated and vehement.

Throwing the body's weight on the backward leg (Fig. 15), gives postures which more properly express passive sensations or indecision, such as:

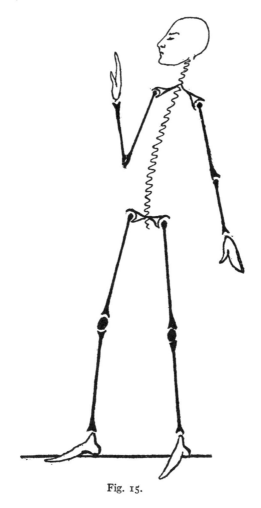

Fig. 15.

Ignorance.	Stupefaction.	Doubt.	Meditation.
Anxiety.	Hesitation.	Negation.	Repugnance.
Astonishment.	Fear.	Scorn.	Terror.

The force of expression of the above attitudes is much increased by bending the leg which supports the body (Fig. 16).

To sum up: simply standing, the body resting on both legs,

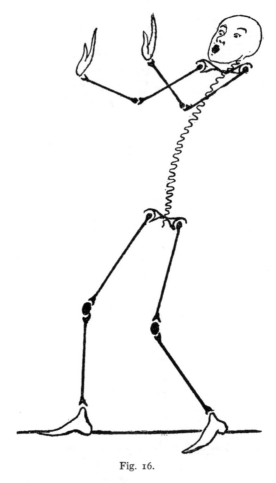

Fig. 16.

the feet together or separated on an even line, is a position which expresses states of inferiority, of indifference, or of controlled sentiments; but as soon as one is called on to manifest a passion, an act of will, or intense emotion, actors are strongly urged to carry the body on one leg, more or less bent, in front, or rear, according to the nature of the sentiment to be expressed. These movements forward and backward offer a large field of resources in dramatic art.

Another advantage the artist will gain from this habit will be to always have one leg free — ready to move elsewhere.

Standing, for instance, on the right leg, before the end of the sentence, he can turn the left leg in the most favorable manner to start in a given direction, thus avoiding the disagreeable shuffling of the feet which is often to be deplored at the theater.

Please note that it is not sufficient merely to read these lessons; they can only be of real value when the artist himself practices the designated movements in the positions which have been pointed out.

The Walk

It is quite difficult to walk in a fit and proper manner on the stage. It is hardly possible to teach an actor how he should walk. Some people are naturally limber and springy and walk well without ever thinking about it. Others are heavy, stiff, awkward in moving their legs, and walk badly.

Instead of saying that one must learn how to walk, say rather that natural faults which cause an improper walk must be corrected. The best way, and perhaps the only way, is to practice with persistence and perseverance the beginning exercises for dancing which have been mentioned before.

As to improper walks purposely used to characterize an impersonation, notice what was previously said about standing (see Figs. 9 and 10), spreading and bending the legs. Holding the legs stiff produces a hesitating and jerky walk useful in portraying old soldiers or old rheumatics.

To give the impression of walking in mud, step on the toes, placing each foot reluctantly, with the air of picking out the cleanest spot. Note that the body is always carried by the forward foot (Fig. 17).

To walk stealthily, step in the same way on tip-toe, but with this difference: that the body does not rest on the forward foot until this has been placed entirely on the ground. Also, the eyes, instead of examining the ground, are fixed on the point to be approached (Fig. 18).

To enter, to cross the stage, to turn, to keep in the back-

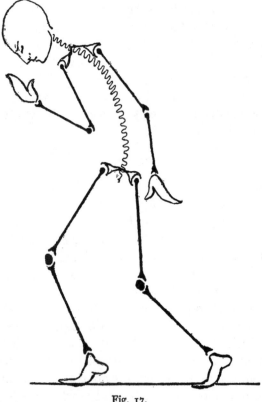

Fig. 17.

ground, to leave, are movements capable of infinite variations, but they can only be studied and indicated in actual practice on the stage. Nevertheless, here is a useful exercise for the purpose of learning to turn on the stage and to move easily in all directions. Address yourself to all the pieces of furniture in the room, going from one to another in turn, but give yourself tests more and more difficult, until you succeed in going with ease

from a selected spot to one diametrically opposite. While re-
peating this exercise you will especially appreciate the advantage of always poising the body's weight on one leg, as in this
position you are always ready to move. For violent movements

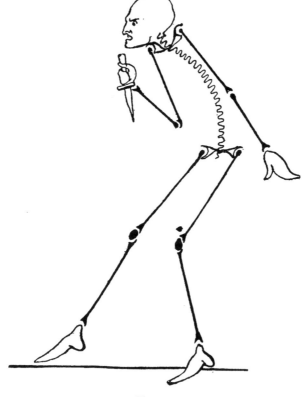

Fig. 18.

like running, jumping, etc., the only point is that they should
be done on the toes. To kneel by bending both knees at once
means that, at a certain moment, you will lose your balance
quickly and strike the floor with a noise. This is only useful
for comic effects. To kneel gracefully, take a step in advance,
throw the weight of the body on the forward foot, and sustain
it there until the backward knee has touched the floor (Fig. 19).

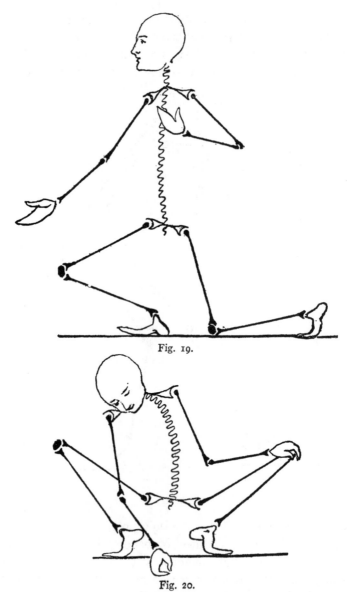

Fig. 19.

Fig. 20.

To pick up an object, if you bend both limbs at once, you have at a certain moment, a very ugly posture (Fig. 20), especially for a woman.

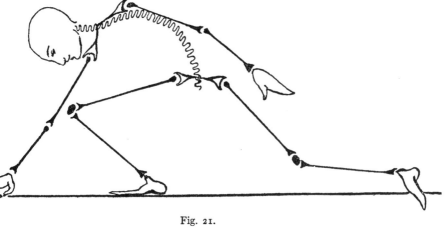

Fig. 21.

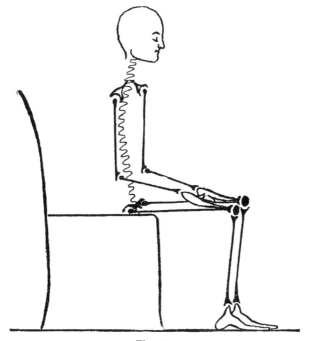

Fig. 22.

Proceed as in kneeling, that is, throw all the weight on the
bending knee (Fig. 21).

Sitting postures are too numerous to be completely analysed. But some general observations may prove useful.

Avoid rigidity or stiffness of the body and identical positions of both limbs.

Avoid spreading the knees far apart.

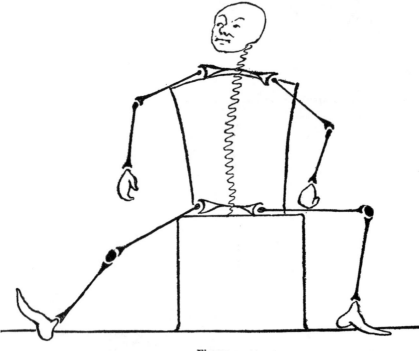

Fig. 23.

To sit very straight, elbows tight to the body, knees on the same line and pressed close together expresses:

      Timidity.   Respectful waiting.

To sit on the extreme edge of the seat gives the same expressions raised to a comical degree (Fig. 22).

To sit, with body twisted, legs wide apart (Fig. 23) indicates:

    Vulgarity.   Don't care.   Impudence.

To sit, legs wide apart, chest forward and elbows resting on your knees, gives the picture of a rough person without education.

The two last suit only very common characters.

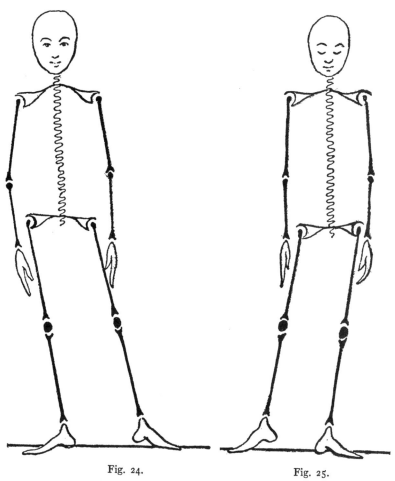

Fig. 24.   Fig. 25.

The study of salutations will be taken up here only from the angle of leg movements, leaving out consideration of familiar, contemptuous and patronizing bows, etc., whose peculiarity is that the legs have no part in them.

A formal bow from a man consists of a preparatory movement, and a bowing movement. With his feet on a line, (it was
mentioned that this posture signifies respect), the preparatory

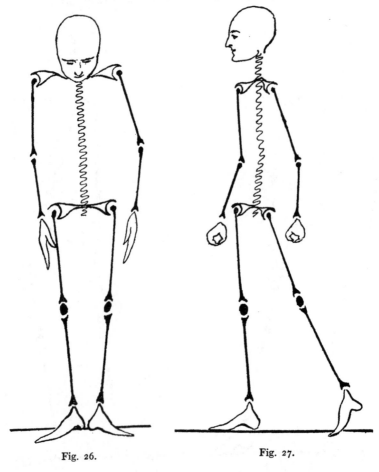

Fig. 26.   Fig. 27.

movement consists in separating the feet about ten inches (Fig.
24) and transferring all the weight to the leg just moved (Fig.
25). The salutation consists in drawing up the free foot to that
supporting the body and lightly clicking the heels (Fig. 26).
Bending the head occurs immediately after the heels are drawn

together. The degree of respect implied by the bow depends on the degree of the movement of the head.

The preparatory movements are exactly the same for a woman as for a man. (See Figs. 24 and 25.)

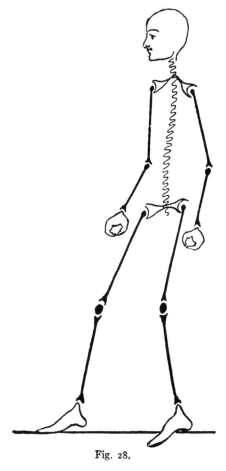

Fig. 28.

To make a curtsey, take one step to the rear with the free foot (Fig. 27), bring all the weight on this latter (Fig. 28), bend this leg (Fig. 29), and to conclude, straighten up by drawing back the leg that was in front.

The chest and head should remain erect. The degree of respect is expressed by the greater or lesser flexion of the leg supporting the body. Notice that a man in saluting, moves his body once, a woman twice. A woman should not bend her head or chest except when she salutes from a sitting position. At

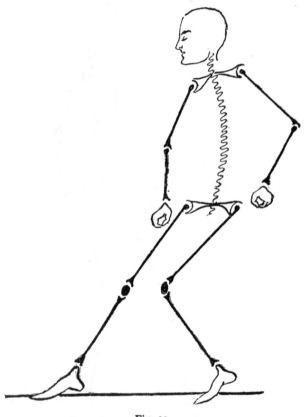

Fig. 29.

any time, being seated, she can make certain bows with the head or upper part of the body, but then the legs do not stir.

A comic bow is executed by a series of backward kicks, in stamping hard on the floor, each kick alternating with a violent movement of the head and body. This is the countryman's bow and a peasant woman may use it also. Still if she is young and pretty, she had better use the soubrette's curtsey, which is made this way:

First time: the left foot is moved behind, the whole weight

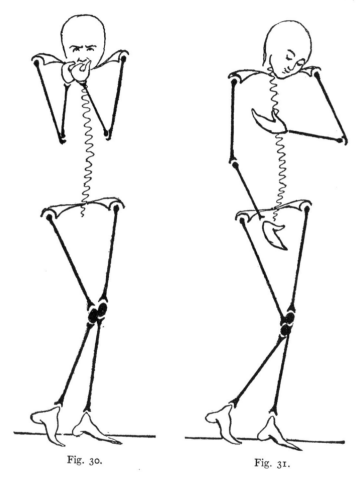

Fig. 30.   Fig. 31.

of the body borne by the right leg and both legs are bent at the same moment.

Second time: The legs are straightened and the left foot brought back to its first position, near the right one.

The whole curtsey is made in two quick movements. The

head and shoulders remain straight. Note that the weight of the body is supported by the same leg throughout.

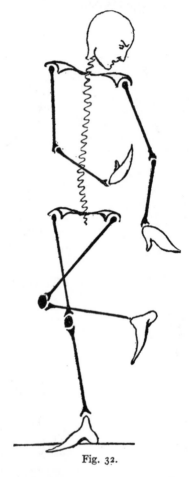

Fig. 32.

Several very expressive movements can be executed by the legs such as:

Both legs pressed close together, one knee slightly covering the other (Fig. 30), completes postures expressing:

All physical suffering.	Shame.
Especially from cold.	Humility.

The same, the legs not quite so close, indicates modesty (Fig. 31).

Same position, one leg raised (Fig. 32), covering the other expresses:

Fear of a dog.   Of a blow aimed low.

Fear of danger coming from low down

Positions of the Feet.

The act of wiping the feet expresses, by suggestion:

It is muddy.   It is raining.
I am soaking wet.   It is frightful weather.

To tap with the foot signifies:

Impatience.   Is he never coming?
Irritation.   Will it ever be finished?

To stamp the foot completes the following expressions:

I am furious.   I insist.   I take.
It has fallen down. I will.   I ruin.
              All interjections.

To advance the foot, then draw it back, signifies:

I hesitate.   I do not dare.   I am afraid.

Positions of the Body

To bend the body (Fig. 33), assists the expression of:

Timidity.   Dissimulation.
Hypocrisy.   Physical suffering.
Premeditation.   Humility.
Old age.   Remorse.
Self-distrust.   Terror.
Shame.   Apprehension.

The abdomen drawn in intensifies the expressions signified by the bowed body.

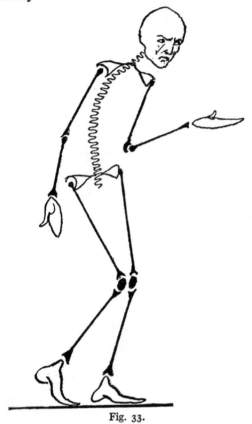

Fig. 33.

The body turned means (Fig. 34):

Well-being.	Will.
Security.	Defiance.
Insolence.	Pride.
Arrogance.	Revolt.

The abdomen prominently displayed with a kind of complacency happily completes the expressions signified by the turned body.

Body bent to right or left signifies (Fig. 35):

Complacency.   Deference.
Coquetry.   Wish to please.

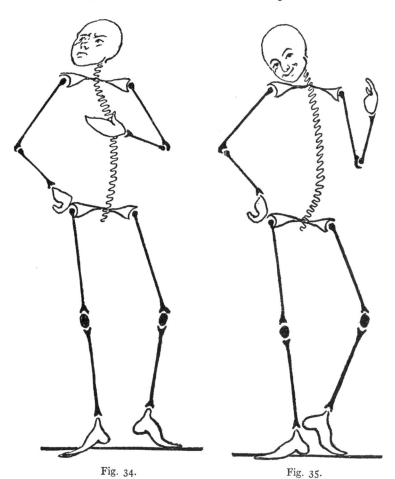

Fig. 34.   Fig. 35.

Body turned around (Fig. 36), signifies:

Attention.   Prudence.   Fear.   Distrust.

Positions of the Abdomen

There is no consideration here of the size of the abdomen, but solely its use in expression, and it is a great mistake to think the

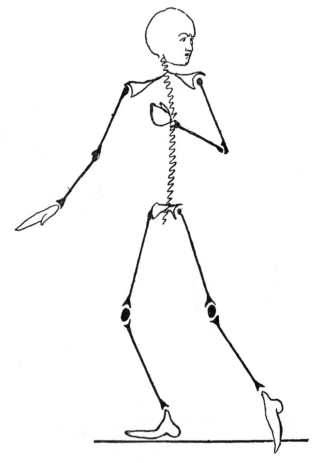

Fig. 36.

largest are the most eloquent. Rather is the contrary the fact. Only by the way the abdomen is held can it be made to express something. There are but two movements. Pushing it for-

ward. Drawing it in. (Described under Figs. 33 and 34.)
An actor would make a great mistake to neglect these two
movements for they produce very quick and characteristic
effects. In the theater nothing escapes the public's eye; each

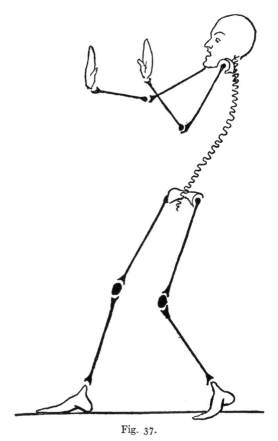

Fig. 37.

logical movement, no matter how slight, is immediately grasped,
understood and appreciated.

POSITION OF THE SHOULDERS

When drawn back they force the abdomen forward (Fig.
34); this movement rounds out and strengthens the expressions

given by the turned or twisted body and prominent abdomen.

Carried forward, they draw the abdomen in: part of the posture of the bent body and hollow abdomen (Fig. 33).

The shoulders raised and carried forward, the head sunk, produces one of the most expressive and most frequently used postures on the stage (Fig. 37). It aids in depicting a range of emotions from the tenderest sentiments to the most extreme and varied. It signifies, above all, excess of sensation, whatever be its nature:

Admiration.	Love.	Extreme suffering.
Ecstasy.	Prayer.	Ravishment.
Desire.	Extreme joy.	Despair.
Shame.		Stupefaction.
Fury.		Horror.

Quick elevation of one or both shoulders helps to express:

Come now!	Mockery.
That's absurd!	Disparagement.
What a joke!	How silly!

The same movement, more slowly done, expresses:

I don't condescend to answer. I am sorry for that.

Shoulders raised high and held there a moment (Fig. 38), give the following expressions:

I doubt. I ignore. Perhaps. It's possible.

Shoulders raised and rounded:

But it's heavy! What a burden!

Light alternate movements of both shoulders forward and back with pouting expression of a spoiled child:

I sulk. I pout. No, I don't want to.
I don't want to know anything.

The same, but very languishing:

I feel very queer. I don't know what ails me.

The same, violently:

I struggle.   I open a path for myself.   I free myself.

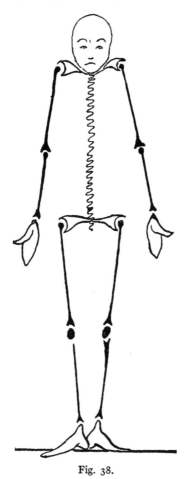

Fig. 38.

Positions of the Arms

Hanging beside the body is a natural position to accompany the following expressions:

Indifference.   Repose.   Low spirits.   Lassitude.

Swinging the arms:

Heedlessness.   Thoughtlessness.   Ease.

Held out from the body:

A ridiculous position which goes well with similar position of the legs. (Fig. 9.)

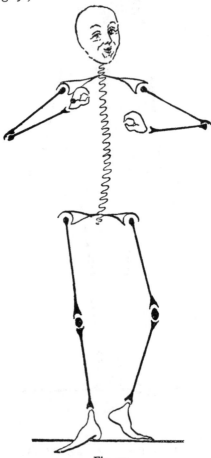

Fig. 39.

The forearms raised, elbows sticking out (Fig. 39):

Affectation.   Desire to appear gracious.
Mannerism.   Comical empty-headedness.

Arms resting on the hips (Fig. 40):

Position of waiting, particularly useful for women.

Thumbs in armholes of the vest (Fig. 41):

Assurance.   Independence.   Gay humor.   Self-content.

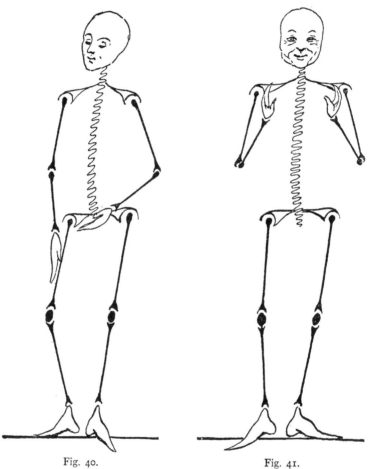

Fig. 40.   Fig. 41.

A hand on the hip or arm akimbo (See Fig. 11). To be harmonious and balanced, this position requires the right hand to be used when the body is supported by the right leg. Expressions: Waiting.   Indifference.

The hand on the hip with more or less marked turning of the head expresses:

Arrogance. Self-sufficiency. Bravado. Challenge.

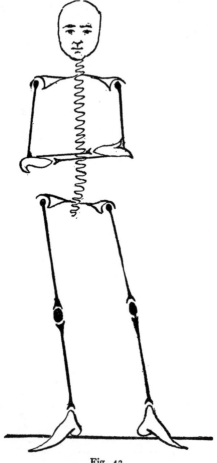

Fig. 42.

In principle, the hand should rest on the hip on the side opposite the action, but note that the breaking of this rule gives by opposition more force to the expression of disdain and insolence (Fig. 34).

Both hands on the hips, whichever leg supports the body,

gives the same expressions as the preceding attitudes, but less pleasing because symmetrical.

Both arms folded on the chest, one supporting the other (Fig. 42), position of:

Expectancy.   Reflection.

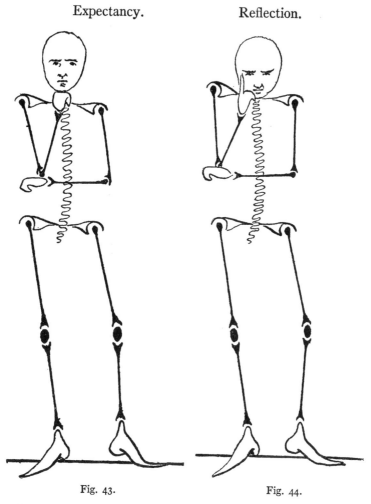

Fig. 43.   Fig. 44.

One arm on the chest supporting the other which holds the chin (Fig. 43), means:

Preoccupation.   Intellectual effort.

Same position of arms, one hand against the cheek, index finger on the temple (Fig. 44):

Profound meditation.   Perplexity.
Difficult problem to solve.

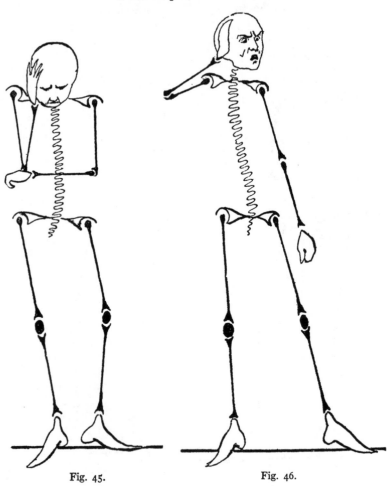

Fig. 45.   Fig. 46.

Same position, the open hand holding the head (Fig. 45):

Anguish.   Extreme embarrassment.
Moral tortures.   Tempest inside the head.

Note that this series of graded positions draws its eloquence from the progressive inclination of the head which seems to

Fig. 47.

grow heavier under the almost physical weight of a thought of graver and graver uneasiness.

One hand pressing the slightly turned head, the other arm straight, a trifle apart from the body (Fig. 46):

What shall I do?	All is lost!
My head bursts!	Despair.
What will become of me?	It will drive me crazy!

Both hands grasping the head (Fig. 47): The foregoing expressions, but much emphasized.

Both hands, open or closed, pressing the temples, the head thrown backwards (Fig. 48): The same expression in their greatest intensity.

Fig. 48.

The arms crossed on the chest really signifies only:

Moment of inaction.　　Self-confidence.

However, in certain cases it may mean:

To face a danger bravely.　　To brave a threat.

Hanging close to the body goes with the posture of both feet in the same line. (See Fig. 8.)

The arms bent and pressed to the body. This movement

completes the expressions given by the legs drawn together, one knee covering the other. (Figs. 30 and 33.)

Clasping the hands behind the back signifies:

Sentiment of security.   Sense of being at home.

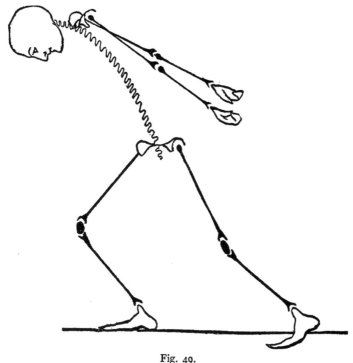

Fig. 49.

To put the hands in the pockets is an improper attitude.

Stretched behind, one leg and the upper part of the body carried forward (Fig. 49):

To draw.   To pull.

Stretched forward, same position of legs and body (Fig. 50):

To push.   To push away.   To drive back.

In a circle above the head (Fig. 51):

To dance.   Let the feast begin.

Arm crooked and presented on the side (Fig. 52):

To offer the arm.

Like a basket in front (Fig. 53):

To carry an armful.

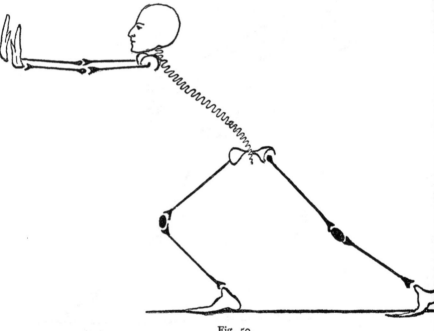

Fig. 50.

Same position, closer to the body, one elbow raised higher than the other (Fig. 54):

To hold a child in one's arms, and, by suggestion:

A child.   A mother.

One arm crooked at the level of the head (Fig. 55):

To threaten some one with a back stroke.

The forearm raised horizontally to the level of the brows and the glance passing under it (Fig. 56):

Fear of a blow on the head.   Confusion.   Shame.

An arm bent, the elbow thrust violently backward:

Leave me in peace now.   Let go of my arm.

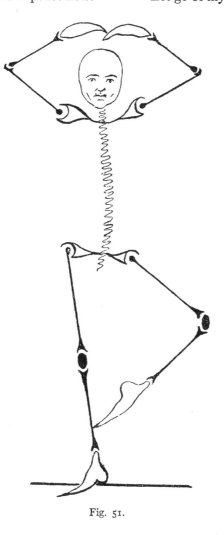

Fig. 51.

The same movement carried out alternately by both arms:

I made my elbows work.   I extricated myself.
Good riddance.

Flapping the elbows like wings signifies:

>Some one who has wings.

Other arm movements are necessary to complete gesticulations of the hands which will be studied later.

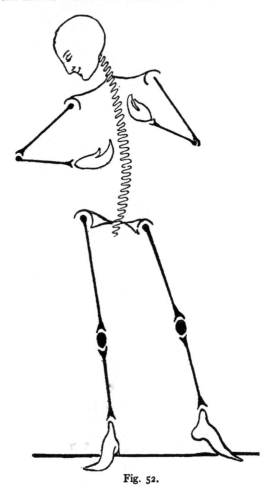

Fig. 52.

Positions of the Head

Raised (Fig. 57). This movement assists in expressing all shades of the proper or exaggerated sense of one's own worth.

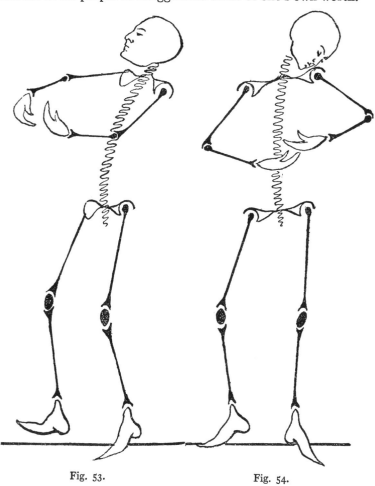

Fig. 53.

Dignity.
Pride.
Will.

Fig. 54.

Assurance.
Bravery.

Raised and slightly tilted backward (Fig. 58): exaggeration of preceding qualities and also:

Arrogance.   Insolence.   Defiance.   Revolt.

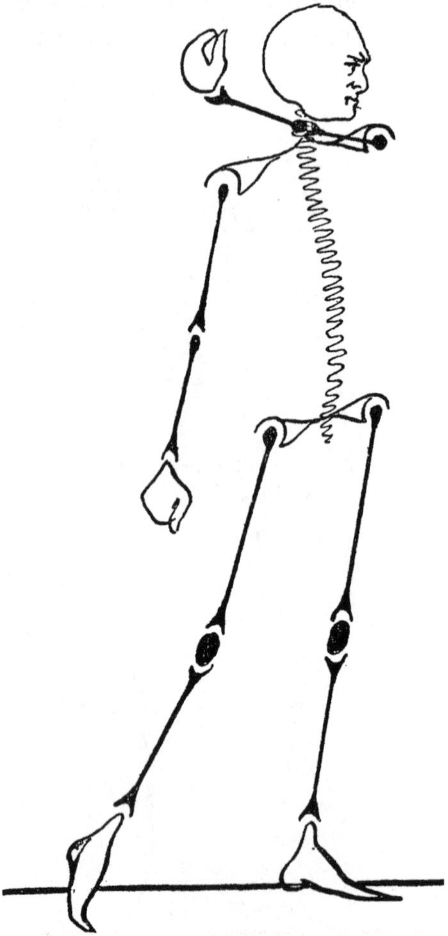

Fig. 55. 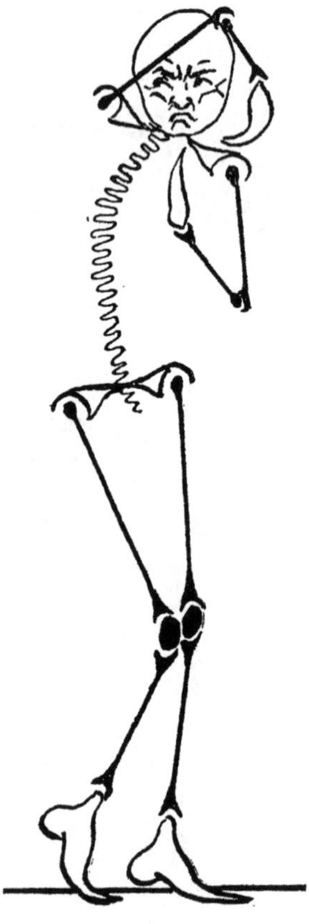   Fig. 56.

This movement completes the pose of Fig. 34.

Tilted farther back, with abandon, eyes closed (Fig. 59):

Weakness.   Suffering.
Faintness.   Exhaustion.

Leaned toward the shoulder (Fig. 60):

<table>
<tr><td>Grace.</td><td>Desire to please.</td></tr>
<tr><td>Coquetry.</td><td>Affectation.</td></tr>
</table>

Much bent sideways:

<table>
<tr><td>Sleep.</td><td>Surrender.</td></tr>
</table>

Fig. 57.

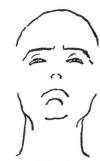

Fig. 58.

Fig. 59.

Fig. 60.

Turned (Fig. 61):

<table>
<tr><td>Attention.</td><td>Observation.</td></tr>
</table>

The same with the shoulders raised (Fig. 62):

<table>
<tr><td>Suspicion.</td><td>Fear.</td></tr>
<tr><td>Apprehension.</td><td>Terror.</td></tr>
</table>

Turned and bent back (Fig. 63):

Insolence.   Hauteur.

Defiance.   Bravado.

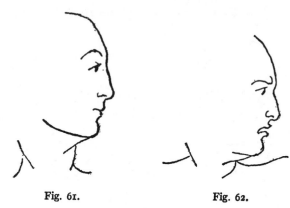

Fig. 61.   Fig. 62.

 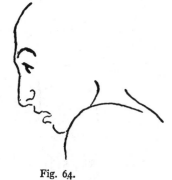

Fig. 63.   Fig. 64.

Head sunk and leaning forward (Fig. 64):

Wildness.   Preparation for a fight.

Ferocity.   Sensation of a beast at bay.

Sunk and thrown backward (Fig. 65):

Stupefaction.   Terrifying vision.   Horror.

Straight and thrust forward (Fig. 66): The study of this movement is specially recommended as it is one of the most expressive. It serves to depict the lightest sentiment of politeness

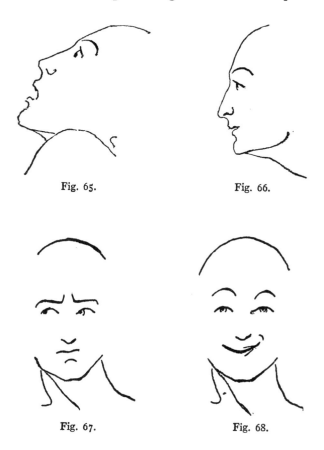

Fig. 65.   Fig. 66.

Fig. 67.   Fig. 68.

and also the most violent passions. Moreover it completes nearly all the expressions implied by raising the shoulders. (See Fig. 37.) Furthermore this movement always indicates a desire, an act of volition.

Straight, upright, carried to one side (Fig. 67):

To listen.

Straight, upright, with a slight change in the direction of the look (Fig. 68):

To hear.

Straight and drawn back (Fig. 69):

Horror.	Vexation.	Scorn.
Disgust.	Repugnance.	

Fig. 69.

Speaking Expressions of the Head

Light forward movement:

Yes.	Impertinent.
Familiar greeting.	Waiting.

Decided inclination, including the bust:

| Acquiescence. | Ceremonious bow. |

Inclining the head over the shoulder:

| Consent. | Friendly bow. |

The same movement, but slower, including the bust; the same expressions with more gravity.

Light forward movements, repeated:

Yes, yes!	Encouragement.
Very well!	Approbation.

Turning the head from right to left and reverse:

No.

Wagging the head first towards one shoulder, then the other:

What a misfortune!	Desolation.
How sad that is!	Disapprobation.

The same with the head turned backward:

Isn't it beautiful?	Delirium.
Enthusiasm.	Ecstasy.

Slow movement of the head up and down, down and up, with the shoulders included, following the motion of the respiration:

Alas!

DETAILED ANALYSIS OF THE MUSCLES
OF THE FACE

The Cheeks

Closely drawn in or hollow (Fig. 70):

Thinness.   Misery.   Illness.

Less closely drawn in, but with lengthening of the face (Fig. 71):

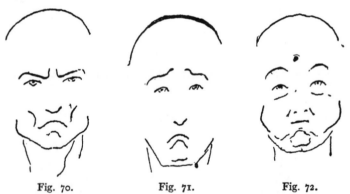

Fig. 70.   Fig. 71.   Fig. 72.

To have met a loss.   To be ridiculed.
To feel sheepish.   Trapped.

Puffed out (Fig. 72):

Fat.   Prosperity.   Feeling well.
Comic importance.   Chubby.

The same, chewing:

To have the mouth full.   To be a pig.

Raised towards the cheek-bones and wrinkled under the eyes (Fig. 73):

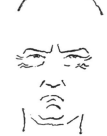

Discontent.
Disparagement.
Dislike.
This is bad.
You give me a pain.
Scorn.
I am disillusioned.
Bitter criticism.
That turns out badly.

Fig. 73.

Notice that this movement of the cheeks begins the action of weeping.

THE NOSE

Dilation of the nostrils (Fig. 74):

To scent.   To smell something.

This movement is also involuntarily made in many strong emotions.

Fig. 74.

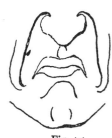

Fig. 75.

Drawing up the sides of the nose (Fig. 75):

That smells badly.   I despise you.
My business does badly.   Fi, fi, that's base.
I smell a trap.   It is disgusting.
I must be on my guard.   All injuries.

Notice that the physical disgust inspired by an unpleasant odor and the moral disgust caused by some fact both manifest themselves in the same manner.

THE TONGUE

Thick and outside the mouth:

> To dangle.

Drawn in and out rapidly:

> Mischief.

Licking the lips:

> Greediness.   Temptation.

Placed in a corner of the mouth and bitten:

> Comic application.

THE JAWS

Measured movements:

> To chew.

Quick little movements, the front teeth meeting and the lips drawn back:

> To nibble.

And by suggestion:

> A mouse.   **A rodent.**

Opening and closing with vigor:

> To bite.

Chattering, the lips parted:

> To be cold.   To shiver.

Teeth closed, lips drawn back, violent head movements:

> To tear prey to pieces.

To show the teeth by opening the lips and pointing to them with a finger:

> The teeth.

With the lips closed and drawn in, to make the jaws work on nothing means:

He has no more teeth.

The jaws closed forcefully, the lips stretched in a grin:

Anger.   Desire for revenge.

Primitively, no doubt: Desire to bite some one.

The jaws open, lips drawn far back:

Ferocity.   A wild beast.

The jaws wide open, lips natural:

Yawning.   Need of sleep.   Ennui.

Notice in the following movements, which have great power of expression, the curious difference of meaning which results

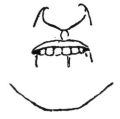

Fig. 76.

Fig. 77.

from the pushing forward or drawing back of the lower jaw.

Biting the lower lip, causing the drawing back of the lower jaw (Fig. 76):

Disappointment.   I made a fool of myself.

Another difficulty.   How shall I get out of this?

Same thing, smiling (Fig. 77):

What luck!   Is she pretty!

Haven't I been smart!

In a general sense:

Windfall!   Unhoped-for results.

The principle of this biting may be precaution taken not to betray a disappointment or a joy. Notice that when the lower jaw is drawn in it is never possible to have a wicked expression. It is always kindly even in ill humor.

Fig. 78.

Biting of the upper lip, causing the lower jaw to protrude (Fig. 78):

I am enraged!	What bad luck!
I am vexed!	They shall pay for this!
How to get even?	I am full of hate.

It is impossible to smile and the whole expression is strongly marked with cruelty.

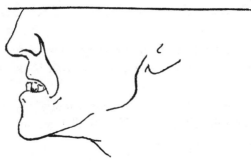

Fig. 79.

The jaws half-open, lower jaw thrust far forward (Fig. 79):

Sarcasm.	Suspicion.	Disgust.	Fury.
Reproach.	Threats.	Injuries.	Severity.

Dropping the lower jaw (Fig. 80):

Ecstasy.	Joy.	Ignorance.
Fear.	Stupor.	Ruination.

Fig. 80.

THE EYEBROWS

As the play of the eyebrows governs all the movements produced on the forehead, the former alone will be considered.

It is impossible to give too much attention to the following movements as they are of capital importance in pantomime.

Raising the eyebrows, thus forming horizontal wrinkles on the forehead (Fig. 81):

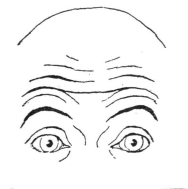

Fig. 81.

Prayer.
Joy.
Gayety.
Admiration.
Ecstasy.
Fascination.
Shame.
Cowardice.
Astonishment.
Ignorance.
Lack of intelligence.

The same movement but more emphasized (Fig. 82):

Fig. 82.

Stupefaction.   Extreme joy.
Fright.   Burst of laughter.
Physical torture.   Dumfounded.

Fig. 83.

Note that all these expressions represent purely instinctive emotions, absolutely lacking in volition or in action of the mind.

Eyebrows dropped, forehead smooth (Fig. 83):

Dignity.   Firmness.
Gravity.   Mental activity.

The eyebrows dropped and drawn together, causing two vertical lines at the base of the forehead:

Covetousness.	Uneasiness.	Severity.
Discontent.	Anger.	Will.
Sadness.	Thought.	Anxiety.

Drawn close together, causing several vertical lines (Fig. 84):

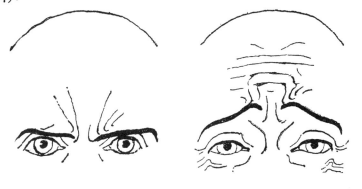

Fig. 84.	Fig. 85.
Great turmoil of mind.	Moral torment.
Terrible apprehension.	Revolt.
Heavy boredom.	Fury.
Anguish.	Fierce resistance.

In general: the extreme limits of combativeness.

Note that these last movements express only sentiments where intelligence and above all the will are powerfully exerted.

To sum up, the eyebrows have but two movements, raising, which brings horizontal lines on the brow; and lowering and drawing them together, which causes vertical lines on the base of the forehead.

These movements are so closely linked to the feelings which bring them into view that when one is a prey at the same time to two contrary emotions they show on the forehead by wrinkles in opposite directions (Fig. 85).

For example: we feel great physical suffering (which is registered by horizontal lines); but at the same time we will to react against this suffering (this effort of will is revealed by vertical lines).

We see a clown whose antics excite our gayety (horizontal lines) but at the same time the dangerous stunts he performs cause us apprehension (vertical lines). We are told something which fills us with amazement (horizontal lines) but at the same time causes the suspicion that perhaps we are being fooled, which irritates us (vertical lines).

Invariably these double feelings betray themselves by contrary corrugations.

THE LIPS

Pinched (Fig. 86):

    Prudishness.   Vexation.   Displeasure.

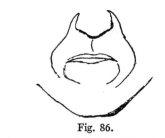

Fig. 86.

Fig. 87.

Drawn in (Fig. 87):

    Controlled anger.   Wickedness.

Fig. 88.

Drawn in and slightly disclosing the teeth (Fig. 88):
Desire to do harm.　　Cruelty.　　Hate.

Fig. 89.

Half-open, corners drooping a little (Fig. 89):
Disdain.　　　　Disparagement.

Fig. 90.

Half-open, corners drawn down (Fig. 90):
Suspicion. Disgust. Injuries. Bitterness. Physical suffering.

Notice that in this expression the lips are parted because turning up the nostrils draws up the upper lip.

Fig. 91.

Closed, only one corner depressed (Fig. 91):

He wants to fool me.	He lies.
He takes me for an easy mark.	I blame.
I suspect.	I find it bad.

In analyzing the play of the features all movements executed by just one of double organs, such as an eye, a corner of the

Fig. 92.

mouth, an eyebrow, constitute asides. Naturally these signs must be made on the side opposite that occupied by the person spoken of.

Closed, with the lower lip pouted and protruded (Fig. 92):

That's ugly.	That's disagreeable.
I don't like that.	This business means nothing to me.

Fig. 93.

Both lips advanced in a pout (Fig. 93):

To pity.	To pray.	I am stubborn.
To sulk.	To dislike.	I will not yield.

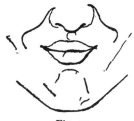

Fig. 94.

Both advanced farther and slightly smiling; though closed (Fig. 94):

A kindly scolding.	Oh! the naughty child.
That's nasty.	Go hide yourself.

Lips puckered as for whistling, and smiling, showing the upper teeth a trifle (Fig. 95):

Coquetry.
Mincing manners.
Affectation.
Desire to please.

Fig. 95.

Fig. 96.

Closed, natural, slightly lifted at the corners (Fig. 96):
Restrained smile.

Corners lifted enough to raise the cheeks (Fig. 97):
To smile.

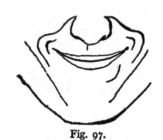

Fig. 97.

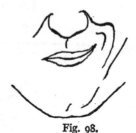

Fig. 98.

The same action, on one side only (Fig. 98):

I lie.	I make game of him.
I fool him.	I state the false to learn the truth.

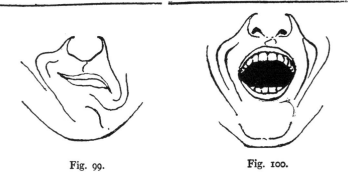

Fig. 99.   Fig. 100.

Raised on one side and drooping on the other (Fig. 99):

Ironical smile.

Raised high; jaws wide open (Fig. 100):

Burst of laughter.

THE EYES

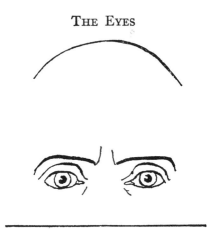

Fig. 101.

Direct look with the head held straight (Fig. 101):
Natural look.

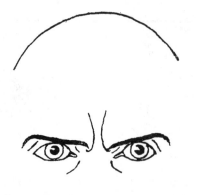

Fig. 102.

Direct look with the head bent forward (Fig. 102):

| Meditation. | Sadness. | Severity. |
| Intellectual effort. | Study. | Ill-will. |

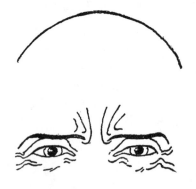

Fig. 103.

Direct look, the head erect with eyelids half-closed (Fig. 103):

Timidity.	Suffering.
This is not plain.	Doubt.
Suspicion.	Unbelief.
Intellectual effort.	Distrust.
Who are they fooling?	Dissimulation.

Notice that when there is a question of intellectual effort, or of a sentiment of distrust, the lower eyelid is the one raised and they are drawn together at the corners while the cheeks rise and wrinkle under the eyes.

On the other hand, when the upper eyelid is relaxed and drooping, the following expressions result:

Kindness.   Fatigue.   Ignorance.

Fig. 104.

One eye half closed (Fig. 104):

He wishes to fool me.   He lies.   I distrust him.

This movement completes expressions signified by drawing down one corner of the mouth (see Fig. 91) and drawing the lips up on one side (see Fig. 98).

Both eyes entirely closed, signifies, according to the gesture or posture:

An effort of memory.   Illness.   Pain.
Shadows, darkness, night.   Sleep.   Death.

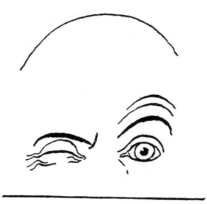

Fig. 105.

One eye closed (Fig. 105):

    There is danger!   Keep your eyes open!

Winking the eyelids rapidly:

    I am stunned.   I see stars!
    What a blow!   I don't know where I am now.

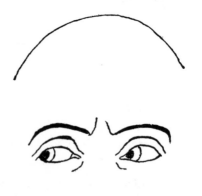

Fig. 106.

Eyes turned to one side, the head not moving (Fig. 106):

    This one.   That one.   I hear.
    I doubt.   I am watching.   Hidden fear.

This expression is confidential.

Fig. 107.

Same movement of eyes, with lids half-closed (Fig. 107):·

I pretend.   I dissimulate.
I spy on.   I betray.
Shame.   Hypocrisy.
Falseness.   Confusion.

Fig. 108.

The eyes cast down (Fig. 108):

Modesty.   Bashfulness.

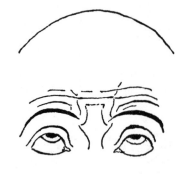

Fig. 109.

A quick upward glance (Fig. 109):

Mon Dieu!	Oh Heavens!
What a scandal!	I call on Heaven to witness!

The same prolonged:

Effort of memory.   Contemplation.   A vision.

A glance around in a circle:

Those.	All of them.
I am watching.	I won't be taken by surprise.

A glance of the eye from below upward:

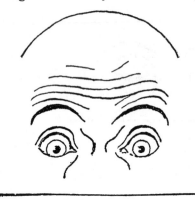

Fig. 110.

To insult.   To defy.
To distrust.
To measure from head
to foot.

The same movement thrown over the shoulder greatly emphasizes these meanings.

Very wide open eyes (Fig. 110):

Anger.	Fright.
Stupefaction.	Fury.
Infatuation.	Extreme physical suffering.

Certainly the eyes play the most important rôle of all the parts of the body, for there is not an instinctive or voluntary dramatic movement which is not accompanied, preceded, and followed by movement of the eyes.

ANALYSIS IN DETAIL OF MOVEMENTS OF THE HANDS

It would be tedious to study all the movements possible to the hands and fingers. Besides, a great number are made unconsciously and have only a vague and indefinite meaning; many only serve the purpose of balancing the body, and of harmonizing or completing poses. It is enough to point out the principles governing those movements which possess a definite meaning. This will give the actor the power to find out for himself, according to his requirements, all shades of each category of expressions.

Hand movements are divided into three classes, namely:

1. Indicative gestures, which point out an object.
2. Descriptive gestures, which measure or delineate an object.
3. Active gestures, which illustrate the action they sketch.

INDICATIVE GESTURES

These designate a person, an object, a spot, a direction.

Excepting those that indicate oneself, they are made with the arm straight out, the first finger pointing, aiming accurately at the object indicated (Fig. 111):

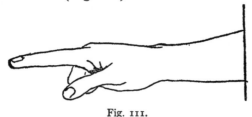

Fig. 111.

You.	This.	Down there.
Him.	Below.	To the right.
They.	Above.	To the left.

The arm bent, first finger pointing to the chest (Fig. 112):

I.   Me.

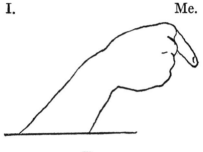

Fig. 112.

The idea of possession and of a larger sense of self is expressed by pressing the open hand on the chest more or less forcefully (Fig. 113):

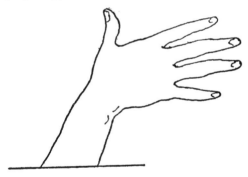

Fig. 113.

Mine.	Which belongs to me.
All my being.	My soul.

This gesture done with both hands gives greater power to the expression.

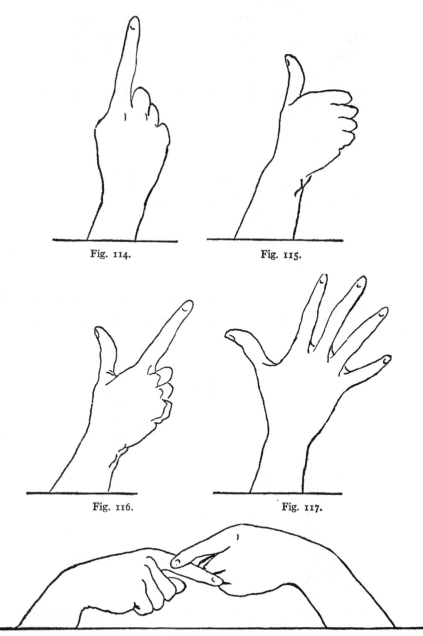

Fig. 114.

Fig. 115.

Fig. 116.

Fig. 117.

Fig. 118.

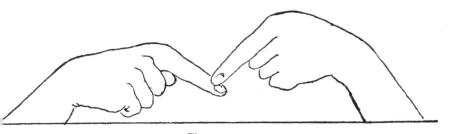

Fig. 119.

Fig. 120.

One only (Fig. 114).
One (Fig. 115).
Two (Fig. 116).
Five. The same done twice: ten. (Fig. 117).
The same repeated several times: many.
The half (Fig. 118).
A little (Fig. 119).
Not that (Fig. 120).

DESCRIPTIVE GESTURES

Their object is to produce the idea of a person or object by
the rapid delineation of its size or shape when this size or shape
is sufficiently characteristic.

The inside of the hand performs the work of outlining sizes and shapes.

These gestures, which require great accuracy, consist in car-

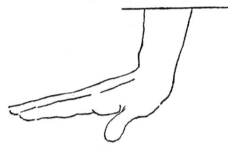

Fig. 121.

rying out in space the exact movements which the hands would make in actually passing over and touching the surface of the

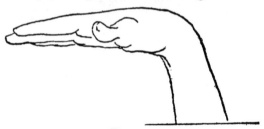

Fig. 122.

object meant. Most descriptive expressions in use require a quick gesture, easy enough to make.

Little (Fig. 121).   Flat.
Large (Fig. 122).   Thin.
Pointed (Fig. 123). Round. Short. Actors are recommended to be very careful when they attempt to enlarge the circle of these descriptive gestures since if these are made more complex there is risk of their not being understood.

ACTIVE GESTURES OF HAND

Hands hanging down, opening and closing several times:

Nervousness.   Beginning of irritation.

Fig. 123.

Hands hanging and clenched:

Irritation.   Desire for revenge.

Fists drawn near to the chest:

Preparation for a fight.

Thrusting out the closed hand and opening it, palm down:

To throw in one's face.   Scorn.

A handful of injuries.

The open hand with fingers spread and palm down, thrust for-

Fig. 124.

ward at the level of the waist and suddenly closing forcefully
(Fig. 124):

I take.   I seize.   I take possession of.

The same movement, but with more violence and the hand closed at the start of the gesture:

I wish.   I hold.   I oppress.
I dominate.   I subjugate.   I destroy.

The same movement, with more flexibility and craftiness, the hand reached out open and then the fingers closed one by one:

To steal.

The hand upright, the palm inside, held at the level of the face, the arm half bent, moving of the tips of the fingers from within outward (Fig. 125):

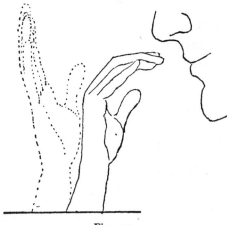

Fig. 125.

Starting from the forehead means a salute.
Starting from the lips means a kiss.
Starting from the heart means a compliment, homage.
Same position, but the movement drawing the tips of the fingers from without towards oneself:

Come.   Approach.   I attract you.

Same movements done on a larger scale with both hands:

All of you come.

Same movement done with first finger only:

Same meaning, but more familiar.

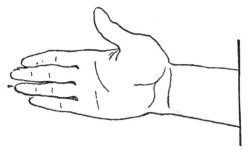

Fig. 126.

Both arms stretched to full length at the level of the shoulders, hands open and palms facing (Fig. 126):

I welcome you.   Kindness.
Come to my arms.   Friendship.

In the same position, the hands starting from the sides and
drawing together in front in a large movement which seems to
include all persons present:

Assemble yourselves together.

Fig. 127.

The opposite movement with palms outward (Fig. 127):

Separate.   Disperse yourselves.   Turn aside.

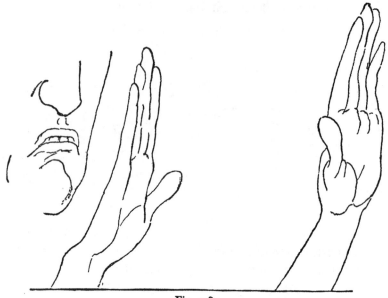

Fig. 128.

One hand upright, near the face, palm out (Fig. 128):

Disgust.	Fright.	I oppose it.
I push away.	Aversion.	I draw away from.
I raise an obstacle.		

The same movement with both hands near the face: the same meanings emphasized.

The same with the arms stretched out: the same meanings but much more vivid.

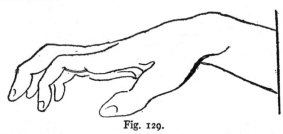

Fig. 129.

Hands advanced horizontally with the fingers separated and hooked (Fig. 129):

Avarice.   Desire to possess.   Temptation to seize.

The same, vertical, with palms facing out:

>   Ferocity.
>   The urge to scratch, to tear, to do mischief.

Up to this point, these active gestures are purely and simply sketches of the actions they signify. Thus they require no fur-

Fig. 130.

ther explanation. But here are others more or less symbolic, for whose origin it is interesting to search.

To offer the hand at the level of the waist, with palm turned nearly upward (Fig. 130):

>   To give the hand.   To beg another's hand.
>   To offer peace.   Allegiance.
>   Proof of confidence.

The actual meaning is:

>   Esteem.   Friendship.   Simple politeness.

The same movement with the hand nearer the body and the palm turned up flat, meant primitively, to be ready to receive an object. Figuratively (Fig. 131):

>   Give me.   I ask.   Grant me.

Carried out further:

I question.   Teach me.
Speak to me.   Explain yourself.

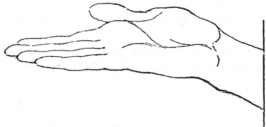

Fig. 131.

The same carried out by both hands:

Same expressions, more grasping, more urgent.

The same position of the hand with a movement from below upward:

To raise.   To sustain.   To support.   To lift.

The same movement, more quickly made:

Get up.   Stand up.   Upright.

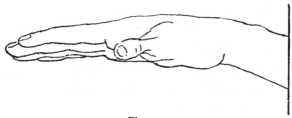

Fig. 132.

Hands horizontal, arms straight, palms down, meant primitively (Fig. 132):

I cover some one.
I shield his head from a blow aimed at him.

Hence the further meaning:

I protect.   I shelter.
I take under my protection.   I defend.

The same, the hands coming from above:

I call down the benefits of heaven.

To bless.   To pardon.

This movement also signifies a covenant:

May misfortune come to this head so dear to me, if I do not fulfill this vow.

On this head, I promise, I swear, I make oath.

Same position of the hands, the arms folded with a slow movement from above down:

To calm.   To appease.   To quiet.

Further meanings:

Silence.   Wait.

Patience.   Be at rest.

Same position, the hands parting horizontally:

Lie down.   Go to bed.

The earth.   A wide expanse.

Fig. 133.

To join the hands in front, palms touching, with the finger tips pointing to the person addressed (Fig. 133):

Primitive significance:

> The image of hands bound together.
> Giving up of natural weapons.
> I am disarmed.   I yield myself.
> I cast myself on your mercy.
> I hope only in your generosity.

Actual significance:

> Pardon.   Mercy.
> I implore.   I pray.

Tips of the fingers pointed towards heaven (Fig. 134):

> Gesture of religious prayer.

The hands joined in the shape of a vase (Fig. 135):

Primitive action of holding water: carried out to mean:

> To gather.
> To make provision.
> The hands full.
> Who holds in his hands.

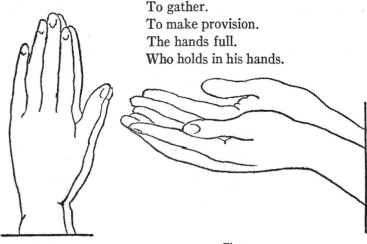

Fig. 134.   Fig. 135.

An open hand in front of one, the palm turned out, finger tips down (Fig. 136):

Primitively: To show the hands. Not to hide anything.
Carried out:

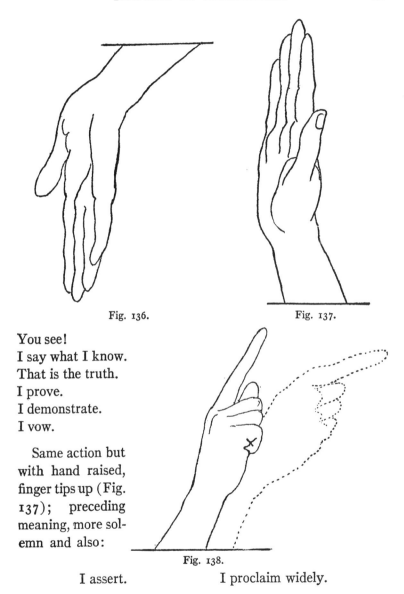

Fig. 136.   Fig. 137.

You see!
I say what I know.
That is the truth.
I prove.
I demonstrate.
I vow.

Same action but
with hand raised,
finger tips up (Fig.
137); preceding
meaning, more sol-
emn and also:

Fig. 138.

I assert.   I proclaim widely.

To shake the index finger near the chin with back of hand
outward, has the primitive significance of (Fig. 138):

Striking with a stick.

Actual meaning:

I threaten you.   You will be punished.
Take care!   You have me to reckon with.

To shake the index finger with the arm stretched out forward, palm of hand outward (Fig. 139):

No, no!   That is not true.
I do not wish.   Denials.

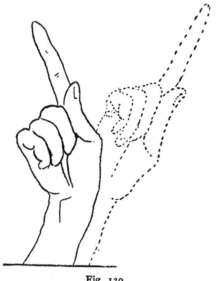

Fig. 139.

Tip of index finger touching the forehead, then quickly pointed outward, palm facing in (Fig. 140):

A thought rises in my brain.   I have an idea.

Same movement, much slower:

I remember.

The two index fingers united:

To become one.   To ally.
To come to an understanding.   To mate.

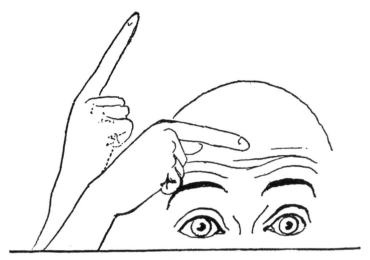

Fig. 140.

To sum up, the following are the principal laws governing the language of the hands:

An absent object is delineated with the palm of the hand as if stroking the imaginary exterior of this object.

Hands upright, palms facing in:

      To call.   To draw.   To welcome.

Hands upright, palms out:

      To remove.   To separate.   To repulse.

Hands horizontal, palms up:

    To ask.   To question.   To raise.   To support.

Hands horizontal, palms down:

To cover.	To protect.	To bless.
To promise.	To soothe.	To pardon.

Hands wide open, carried forward and shown ostentatiously:

To confess.	To prove.
To proclaim.	To demonstrate.

There remain a certain group of gestures whose symbolism is well known and which may be employed in certain situations, in spite of their vulgarity. The main thing is to use them in the right place.

To make fun of anyone.	I am laughing at you.
To make horns.	To run away.
One who wears horns.	To scamper off.
That happens under your nose.	My eye!
Under the chin.	

These gestures are too ordinary to describe. Remember that movements of the hands are very expressive, but the actor is emphatically urged to use them only very definitely and sparingly outside of complementary gestures.

COMPLETE REGISTRATION OF EXPRESSION

The majority of movements which can be executed in a natural manner with the members of the body, and with the muscles of face and hands, have been analyzed in detail, and the meaning of each movement stated. This first work resulted in giving information about the resources people possess. But it is only an inventory. These single movements, studied separately, might be called the words of the language of acting, none of them is absolutely complete in meaning; moreover, their number is limited. It is evident that these movements may be grouped together, associated in various ways to form an infinite number of combinations.

About sixty complete expressions of the principal emotions follow. The most characteristic have been chosen and registered in extreme degree so as to obtain the clearest and most striking signs. It must be understood that each of these expressions is capable of a multitude of shadings. Better still, the greater part of these expressions, simple and complete, can be combined with one another and form double or triple expressions, etc.

Of course it is impossible to point out all feasible combinations, as the number is illimitable. Besides, too great a number of illustrations would have impeded the comprehension of principles.

It is the business of the actor to be thoroughly informed about the movements under his control, their meaning and their force, so that he may bring them together and construct the expressions desired. It is certain that by studying faithfully the preceding expositions he will soon be able to carry out easily and almost without thought, the pantomimic signs for registering all human emotions. It is no more difficult than to join words to form a sentence.

Notice particularly that none of the movements which co-operate to make an expression complete must be omitted. So it is essential to watch at the same time the attitude, the gesture and the facial expression. Sometimes, the physiognomy expresses two emotions at the same time, even contradictory ones like joy and uneasiness, gayety and suffering, but gesture can only convey a single meaning.

The complete expressions shown as examples will be divided into two distinct groups, namely:

First: Expressions stamped by purpose and intelligence.

Second: Passive expressions where will and intelligence are paralyzed for the moment.

The reason for adopting this classification is that always, without exception, it was noticed that these different expressions were characterized by very remarkable signs quite contrary and more or less accented, which are:

For class I — Drawing the eyebrows together produces vertical lines at the base of the forehead.

For class II — Lifting the eyebrows, producing horizontal wrinkles on the forehead.

It would seem that this classification, based on an invariable phenomenon, should facilitate this study. And it might prove of interest to physiologists to strive to find out why a certain state of mind should always and universally manifest itself by the same dramatic lines.

Here are two invaluable rules.

Because of the power of visible action, make only movements that are absolutely necessary.

Acting should consist —

> Always in attitudes.
> Often in facial expressions.
> Rarely in gesticulations.

EXPRESSIONS OF THE ENTIRE HEAD

MARKED BY

WILL AND INTELLIGENCE

Fig. 141.

Modesty.
Timidity.

Greeting.
Acquiescence.

Principal movements:

Bending the head. Drooping the eyelids. (See Fig. 8.)

97

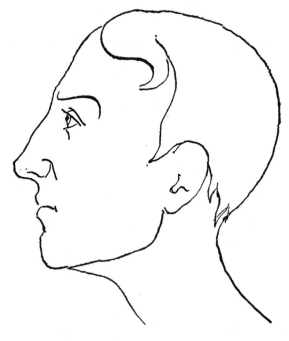

Fig. 142.

Interest.   Curiosity.
Attention.   Activity.

Principal movements. Fixed look. The head moved forward.

(Position Fig. 13.) This movement of the head is one of the most eloquent. It usually indicates a wish, an act of will. It is also the sign of most of the violent emotions.

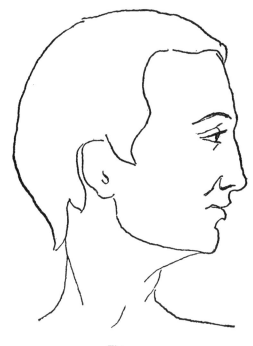

Fig. 143.

Same expressions as the preceding but more indifferent or more familiar.

Principal movement. Turning the head. (Position, Figs. 11 and 12.) This movement is less active than the preceding.

Nevertheless, very happy effects of opposition may be obtained by this turning of the head.

Fig. 144.

Kindness.	Discreet Agreement.
Deference.	Familiar Greeting.
Gallantry.	

Principal movements. The head much turned; the look directed nearly behind. (Position Fig. 36.)

Notice that the sense of grace, of mystery and intimacy are due to the movements of opposition. Kindness is shown by the slightly veiled eye.

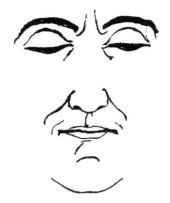

Fig. 145.

Hypocrisy.   Dissimulation.

Principal movement: Looking from between nearly closed
eyelids. (Position Fig. 40.) Note that it is the contradiction
between the half-frowning eyelids (ill-will) and the beginning of
a smile (good-will) which gives the sense of falseness to this
expression.

Fig. 146.

Falseness.	Astuteness.	Deceit.
Treachery.	Malice.	

Position Fig. 33.

Principal movements: Eyelids half-closed. Sideways look. Brows drawn together. Forced smile. Cheeks raised, wrinkling under the eyes. Note same qualities as in preceding expression except that in this last the contradictory movements of the features are more striking.

Fig. 147.

| I lie. | I deceive. |
| I mock. | I jest. |

Principal movements: Smiling on one side only, thus raising the cheek and making the eye smaller. Note that movements carried out by one alone of double features form an " aside."

Any attitude.

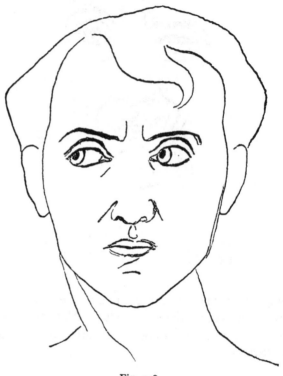

Fig. 148.

To lend the ear.	I listen.
Uneasiness.	I seek to take by surprise.

Principal movements: Head carried to one side and the eyes turned to the side. Position Fig. 12 reversed.

The direction of the look gives significance to this movement. When the eyes look sideways, one tries to hear, one listens; when the glance turns to the audience and a new expression appears on the face, one hears.

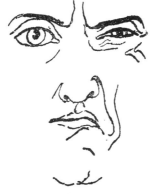

Fig. 149.

He wants to deceive me.   He is lying.
There is something ambiguous.   I have my doubts.

Principal movements: Corner of mouth drawn down. One
cheek raised, partly closing the eye.

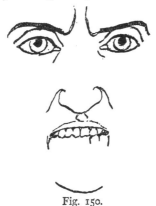

Fig. 150.

Heavens! what a disappointment.   Missed!
I have done a foolish thing.   Unexpected difficulties.

Position Fig. 43.

Principal movements: Biting the lower lip. This act, which
causes the drawing back of the lower jaw, cannot give a malicious look. It expresses also an effort not to show one's spite
or displeasure.

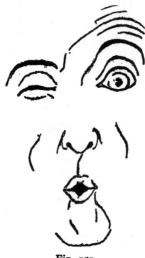

Fig. 151.

The devil!	It's more serious than I thought.
Let's keep our eyes open!	There is danger.
I must look out!	

Position Fig. 46.

Principal movements: One eye quite closed; the other very wide-open. Face drawn down. The mouth puckered up. This is also a confidential expression. The closed eye means dissimulation. The pursed lips controlled surprise. The open eye proclaims danger.

Fig. 152.

| Uneasiness. | Suspicion. |
| Distrust. | They deceive me. |

Position Fig. 15.

Principal movements: Cheeks raised, partly closing the eyes. Brows frowning. Corners of mouth drawn down.

The eyes half shut and looking sideways express disguised mistrust. Frowning brows — irritation and being on the defensive. The drawn down corners of the mouth show bitterness and reproach.

Fig. 153.

Ironic smile.   Raillery.
Disparagement.   Sarcasm.
Scorn.   That's nonsense.

Position Fig. 15.
Movements: One corner of the mouth smiling, the other
drawn down. Upper eyelids slightly drooped. This expression
is quite contradictory. The eyes slightly veiled and the one-
sided smile express condescension. The drawn down corner of
the mouth indicates surmises and disgust. The mocking and
sarcastic significance results from this opposition. This expression is capable of many delicate shadings.

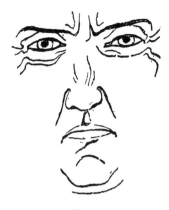

Fig. 154.

Mistrust.   Disapproval.
This is bad.   I do not like this.
Blame.

Position Fig. 15.
Movements: Same as Fig. 152 but with direct look. Here the suspicion, instead of being hidden, is frankly expressed.

Fig. 155.

| What a scandal! | How terrible! |
| I take Heaven to witness! | I call down Divine punishment! |

Position Fig. 16.

Principal movements: The look cast upward; the drawn eyebrows; drooping of lower jaw.

The mouth open as if to shout indicates surprise. Drawing down the brows and the vertical lines of the forehead prove that this surprise excites indignation and the raised look informs heaven of its object.

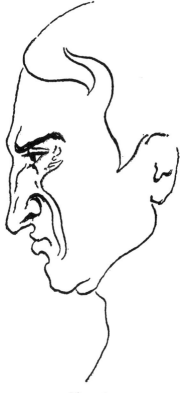

Fig. 156.

Mistrust.   Disgust.
Loss of heart.   Repulsion.

Position Fig. 16.

Movements: Drawing the head backward. Frowning brows. Squinting eyes. Raised nostrils. Corners of mouth drawn down.

The frowning eyebrows express the fighting spirit: the partly closed eyes testify to a displeasing sight: raising the nostrils draws the upper lip into the strongest sign of repugnance: finally, the corners of the mouth drawn downward indicate bitterness and contempt.

In this expression where sight, taste and smell seem disagreeably affected, note that the signs would be the same whether provoked by a mental or physical object. The most prominent characteristic of this expression is the drawing up of the nostrils.

Observe further that the root of these movements of eyes, nose and mouth lies in self-protection, the object being to decrease the disagreeable sensations experienced by the three senses.

There is no reason these signs should ever change as they are useful and logical. This applies to most dramatic manifestations.

Fig. 157.

Same as the preceding, front view.

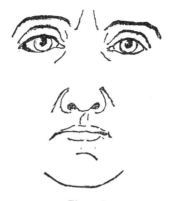

Fig. 158.

Dignity.   Firmness.   Assurance.

Position Fig. 12.

Movements: Head raised.   Brows lowered.   Firm look.
The dignity of the expression depends on the carriage of the
head.

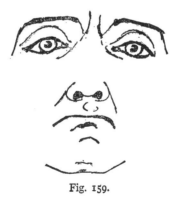

Fig. 159.

Pride.   Insolence.
Authority.   Haughtiness.

Position Fig. 34.

Movements: Head thrown back. Brows severe. Slight protrusion of lower lip. The raised head which allows one to look from above shows the good opinion one has of oneself. The pouting of the lower lip displays disdain felt for others.

Fig. 160.

Deception.	Intellectual activity.
Difficulties to be conquered.	Power of resistance.

Positions Figs. 42 and 43.

Movements: Lowering of brows. Direct gaze. Jaws closed tightly. The severity of the eyes, together with firmness of the mouth characterizes this expression.

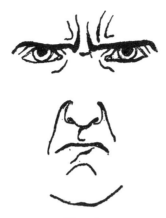

Fig. 161.

Foreseeing danger.	Serious boredom.	I wish.
Tense mind.	Powerful combativeness.	I fight.
Unchanging determination.	Desperate struggle.	

Positions Figs. 43 and 44.

Principal movements: Lowering and drawing together of the eyebrows in vertical lines which accuse strongly. Jaws contracted and corners of mouth drawn down.

The look from beneath the extremely lowered brows acquires depth and somber power. The deeply marked vertical wrinkles indicate exhaustless energy and tenacity of purpose. The closed lips with the corners of the mouth drawn down betray the irritation caused by an obstacle and the firm determination to smash it. The maximum expression of human will results from the union of these signs. The particular shape of the eyebrows is the dominant sign, of great eloquence, in this expression. A fascinating problem to solve would be to learn just why this sign infallibly and constantly accompanies in some degree every act of the human will.

Fig. 162.

Profound discouragement.	Grief.
Moral torture.	Great perplexity.

Positions Figs. 44 and 45.

Movements: Eyebrows drawn far down. Fixed look. Facial muscles relaxed. Head bowed. Line of lips drawn low.

In this expression the eyebrows do not come as near together as in the preceding. The head is bowed, sign of depression: the jaws are parted and all the muscles relaxed, showing weakness of will. It seems as if energy were exhausted and the person more ready to yield to despair than to continue to struggle.

Fig. 163.

Deep anguish.   Despair.   Incurable sorrow.

Same signs as in preceding figure but intensified.   The heavy head bends lower, which gives a deeper and more troubled sadness to the look.

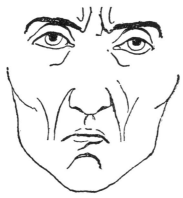

Fig. 164.

Misery.   Physical suffering.
Grief.   Decline.

Positions Figs. 30 and 33.

Movements: Cheeks sunken. Brows frowning. Heaviness of upper eyelids. Corners of the mouth drawn down.

The heaviness of the eyelids, which fall as though weary, produces particularly the expression of grief and discouragement. Still, in spite of the bitterness of the mouth, the vertical wrinkles of the forehead and drawn brows show a habit of effort and exercise of the will.

Note that the last three faces are not of passing expressions, but rather definite conditions to which the muscles seem hardened by misfortune and suffering.

Fig. 165.

Extreme peril.	Desperate situation.
Despair.	Overwhelming horror.

Positions Figs. 46, 47 and 48.

Movements: Violent frown. Extremely wide open eyelids. Dropping the lower jaw.

The eyes are dilated by the sight of fearful danger or a horrible catastrophe. The dropped lower jaw shows a momentary loss of power to move. But the energetic frown indicates that the will has not given up and the person will fight to the bitter end, even without hope.

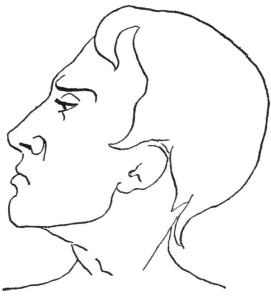

Fig. 166.

Impertinence.   Arrogance.
Challenge.   Revolt.

Position Fig. 34.

Principal movement: The head is turned and thrown back.

This expression is characterized by the backward tilt of the head, but understand that it is much increased by the opposition of the position which compels the turning of the head, and looking at the opponent over the shoulder while the back is almost turned to him. The same expression made directly in front would lose much of its force.

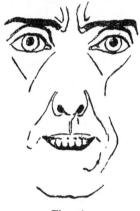

Fig. 167.

Restrained anger.	Desire to harm.
Cruelty.	Ferocity.
Need of vengeance.	Implacable hate.

Position Fig. 13 with the fists clenched.

Principal movement: Biting of the upper lip forcing the lower jaw forward.

It is interesting to compare this expression with Fig. 150 so as to study the curious difference between biting the lower or the upper lip. In the latter action the outline of a smile becomes impossible and the features reflect a strange character of wickedness and cruelty. Nevertheless, this biting of the lip indicates the repression of a violent wave of anger.

Fig. 168.

All the signs of the preceding except that the lip is not pressed by the teeth, the eyes are staring and the brows drawn closer.

Position Fig. 47, but with the fists held in front.

Here fury is not repressed; it is loosed, it bursts forth. The lower jaw protrudes menacingly, the eyes open wide as if to terrorize or fascinate, and the violent contraction of the brows betrays the need of immediate vengeance, the will to conquer, to destroy. The head is thrust far forward, as it is in all excessive emotion where the will is exasperated or crossed. Perhaps this forward thrust of the jaw originates from an instinctive desire to bite.

Fig. 169.

Unloosed fury.   Side view of above.

PASSIVE EXPRESSIONS

Fig. 170.

Attention.   Enticement.
Interest.   Charm.

Principal movements: The head is advanced. Lower jaw is relaxed. The eyebrows are raised.

This expression as a whole indicates that the subject is affected by some outside influence and that he is not active himself.

Fig. 171.

Pleasant sight.   Admiration.
Love.

Principal movements: The head is advanced. The eyebrows
are raised. The dawning smile raises the cheeks.

Attitude: Fig. 14. Advancing the head and raising the eyebrows show that one feels an influence. The whole demon-
strates pleasure, admiration.

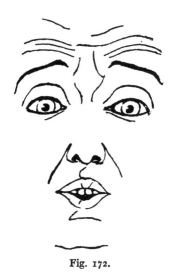

Fig. 172.

Desire.	I wish.
Appetite.	I ask.
Need of possessing.	I beg.

Principal movements: The head is well advanced and tilted backward. The eyebrows are raised and slightly contracted. The lips are pouted.

Attitude: Fig. 14. Here admiration has led to the desire to possess. Extreme desire, which is painful, is manifest in the light frown, while the raised eyebrows indicate the charm experienced or felt; the lips advanced as for a kiss, ask, beg, implore. Then the head advanced and tilted back betrays the ardor and intensity of the passion. Will is not yet manifest, but those feelings that precede and produce it.

Fig. 173.

| Desire to please. | Coquetry. |
| Affectation. | Mannerism. |

Principal movements: Leaning of the head. Raising of the eyebrows. The lips smiling and made small.

Attitudes: Figs. 35 and 39.

The inclination of the head denotes an effort towards a gracious position: the lifting of the brows and the smile betokens self-admiration. Making the mouth small shows desire to please and also that one has delicate and refined taste.

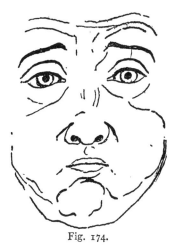

Fig. 174.

Large.   Fat.
Chubby.   Prosperous.

Principal movement: Puffed out cheeks.

Attitude: Fig. 9.

This is merely a descriptive sign to show that someone is large, chubby or in comfortable circumstances.

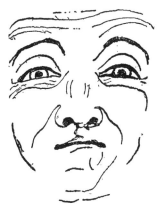

Fig. 175.

Prosperity.   Pleased with oneself.
Satisfaction.   Exaggerated self-importance.

Principal movements: The head thrown back. The eyebrows raised. Expansion of mouth and cheeks.

Attitudes: Figs. 9 and 23.

The raised brows and the smile indicate self-approbation.

Throwing the head back shows the desire to make oneself important. The attitudes suggested as appropriate to this expression reveal the character's vulgarity.

Fig. 176.

Ignorance.   Perhaps.
I don't know.   I haven't an idea about it.

Principal movements: Hunching up the shoulders. Raising the eyebrows high. Corners of mouth drawn down.

Attitude: Fig. 38.

In this expression, the extreme elevation of the eyebrows producing horizontal wrinkles on the forehead, signifies mental blankness for the moment. This sign is voluntarily used in place of speech. The most intelligent man makes use of it. It signifies definitely: On this subject I know nothing at this moment. And by suggestion: I am ignorant. The drawn down corners of the mouth express the displeasure one feels at this ignorance. The hanging arms, with hands showing the palms, confess this ignorance.

The connection between hunching the shoulders and the wish to confess one's ignorance has been looked for in vain. But it can be asserted that this movement always accompanies this feeling and all the world knows and understands it as such.

Besides, this movement of the shoulders especially characterizes feelings of fear. Perhaps it signifies in this last position: I fear to be punished for my ignorance. Do not punish me. Pardon me for not knowing.

Whatever the reason, the expression of ignorance would not be complete without this movement of the shoulders.

Fig. 177.

I hear.   What I hear is agreeable.

Principal movements: The head is carried to one side. Direct forward gaze. Eyebrows raised and mouth smiling.

Attitude: Fig. 12.

The head on one side means to listen, to lend an ear. The forward look at the audience shows that one hears. The upward bend of the eyebrow shows the receipt of an impression and the smile tells that this impression is pleasant.

Compare this with the expression of Fig. 148, which merely hears.

Fig. 178.

Is she pretty!   What a godsend.
I got out of that well.   Unexpected joy.
What luck!

Principal movements: Biting of the lower lip. Raising the eyebrows high. Laughing lips and cheeks.

Attitude: Fig. 13.

The lip is bitten to hold in loud exclamations, and the cheerfulness of the countenance indicates the surprise is a happy one. The raised eyebrows of this expression eloquently accentuate this sentiment of joyous surprise.

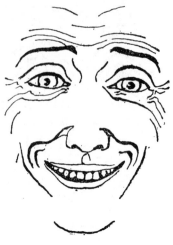

Fig. 179.

Joy.   Contentment.
Gayety.   Physical satisfaction.

Attitudes: Figs. 9 and 10.

Principal movements: The lips are stretched in a grin that pushes up the cheeks into wrinkles under the eyes. The brows are raised high, forming lines across the forehead.

The high elevation of the brows indicates the person is forcibly impressed; and the wide smile shows that it is extremely agreeable. The entire expression manifests a complete satisfaction of physical appetites or being tickled by a sensual and gross idea. The postures suggested complete this impression.

Fig. 180.

Outburst of laughter.

The same movements as the preceding figure carried out to the maximum.

Attitude: Fig. 23.

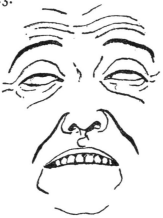

Fig. 181.

Swooning with pleasure.   Excessive feeling.

Principal movements: The head bent back. The eyes cast

upward. The upper eyelids drooping. Eyebrows well raised. The line of the lips stretched taut to disclose the upper teeth.

This expression indicates an excessive sensation. In this condition the muscles left to themselves become set in a sign of the highest degree of feeling. Nevertheless the relaxing of some muscles indicates that the power of sensation, exhausted by too great an effort, is considerably diminished. The high elevation of the eyebrows testifies that emotion has absolute control, excluding the faintest sign of will; the broad smile shows satisfaction, but the convulsed eyes and drooping upper lips betray the excess of the emotion and impotency to sustain it longer.

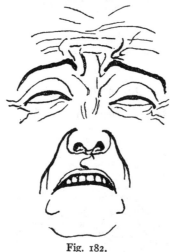

Fig. 182.

Swooning from pain.   Limit of sensation.

The same characteristics as shown in the preceding figure, with the slight difference that vertical lines are found at the base of the forehead mingled with transverse ones which testify to an instinctive and insensible struggle against pain. Also the corners of the mouth being slightly drawn down in spite of their wide stretch shows the sensation is disagreeable. With these modifications, all that was said about the preceding figure applies to this. These two expressions signify extreme emotion; delicate shadings reveal the cause as pleasant or painful.

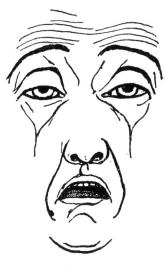

Fig. 183.

To be a sot.	Depravity.
Moral lack.	Absolute dullness.

Attitude: Fig. 10.

Principal movements: Raising of the eyebrows. Drooping of upper eyelids, of lower jaw and all the muscles of the lower part of the face.

Notice that in this expression the signs are not accidental and transitory, but permanent, chronic and definite.

All show of will has disappeared. The raised brows and wrinkling of the forehead indicate the subject is constantly subjected to adverse influences, while the marked relaxation of all the lower muscles of the face proclaims absolute impotence to wish, to act, or to react. It is intellectual death.

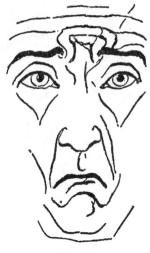

Fig. 184.

| To be crestfallen. | I am thrashed. |
| Caught in a trap. | Duped, beaten, punished. |

Principal movements: Cross wrinkles of the raised and frowning brows. Long face produced by lowering the jaw. Corners of mouth drawn down.

Attitudes: Figs. 8 and 38.

The raised brows and weakness of the lower muscles are the confession of foolishness or of a fault committed; the drooped corners of the mouth and the vertical lines at the base of the forehead signify the regret and discomfort experienced.

Fig. 185.

Regrets.   Remorse.
Shame.   Confusion.

Principal movements: Bowing the head. Crosswise and double movement of the eyebrows. Bitterness of the mouth. Resting the weight of the body on the backward foot.

Attitude: Fig. 15.

The head is bent as if in an effort to hide; this also gives the effect of masking the look. The lips are raised by the turning up of the nostrils and at the same time drawn down at the corners to express the disgust one feels at oneself. The transverse and vertical wrinkles which crisscross on the forehead show both the painful impression received and irritation at finding oneself in such a predicament.

Hunching the shoulders accentuates this expression.

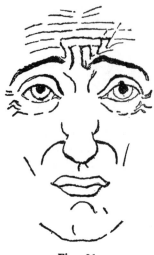

Fig. 186.

To beg.	To implore.
To move to pity.	To complain.

Principal movements: Bowing of the head. Crisscross lines on the forehead. Cheeks raised and wrinkled under the eyes. Lips prominent and pouting.

Attitude: Fig. 33.

All the marks of this expression, the opposing lines of the eyebrows, contraction of the cheeks causing wrinkles under the eyes and on the nose, are characteristic of the desire to weep. They seek to excite pity, to move. The pouting of the lips is both the sign of a kiss and of a plaintive prayer.

Their object is to gain sympathy and kindness. The greater or less degree the head is bowed shows shamed timidity.

Fig. 187.

Sensibility.   To have a heavy heart.
Desire to weep.   Tears held back.

Principal movements: Opposing movements of the brows and
wrinkles on the forehead. Contraction of the cheeks. Corners
of the mouth drawn down.

A variety of attitudes.

The eyebrows raised high forming horizontal wrinkles indicates that one is the victim of violent emotion, while at the
same time the drawing together of the eyebrows causing vertical
wrinkles reveals an effort to resist this emotion, or at least to
suppress showing it. Still, the contraction of the cheeks and the
bitter mouth betray that the emotion is stronger than the will.

Fig. 188.

To weep.   To burst into tears.

The same marks as the preceding figure but much more emphasized. The contraction of the cheeks and of the lower muscles of the face increases, making the eyes smaller, while the
mouth partly opens in a grin.

It is obvious that these movements induced by grief and pain
occur spontaneously and instinctively with the object of relief,
the same as one cries out in pain, yawns when sleepy, laughs
when tickled, etc.

Fig. 189.

Paroxysm of physical pain.

Principal movements: Extreme raising of the eyebrows. Eyes dilated. Mouth grinning and open to let out cries. Contraction of all the facial muscles.

Attitudes: Figs. 16 and 48.

The raised eyebrows covering the forehead with horizontal lines and obliterating vertical ones indicate that sensation has taken full possession and dominates the personality. Will has disappeared, powerless. The distracted being, all at sea, wails sorrowfully, perceiving nothing but immense pain. He scarcely retains a glimmer of intelligence to wish for death. As always with extreme emotions, the hunching of the shoulders accompanies this expression.

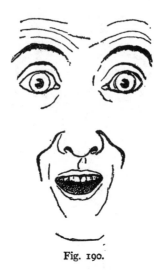

Fig. 190.

Astonishment.

Principal movements: Eyebrows raised high. Mouth open ready to shout. Shoulders raised.

Attitude: Fig. 15.

Sudden sensation, paralysing all the faculties for the moment, is betrayed by the raised eyebrows: the mouth opens to cry out. The half-finished smile in this illustration indicates the surprise is rather agreeable.

Fig. 191.

Stupefaction.

The same movements as the preceding but much more marked.

Attitude: Fig. 16.

This is astonishment at its peak. The whole being is petrified, stupefied. Will and intelligence are entirely gone. In this degree astonishment no longer permits any sign of pleasure. As will be demonstrated, stupefaction can only be joined to a sentiment of fear.

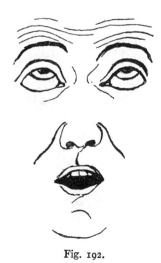

Fig. 192.

Ecstasy.   Rapture.

Principal movements: Elevation of eyebrows; eyes turned towards heaven. Head thrown back. Lower jaw dropped.

Attitude: Fig. 16.

The action of the eyebrows shows one is possessed by an all powerful feeling; the direction of the look indicates this feeling comes from above; the relaxation of the lower jaw shows that will is absent and the individual has entirely forgotten himself.

Fig. 193.

Fright.   Terrifying sight.

Same movements as Fig. 191 with the addition of a contraction of the brows which testifies that the cause of stupefaction is a horrible spectacle or the approach of a frightful danger.

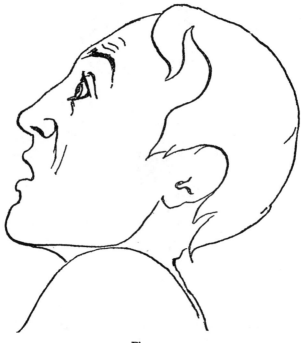

Fig. 194.

Same as the preceding, profile view.

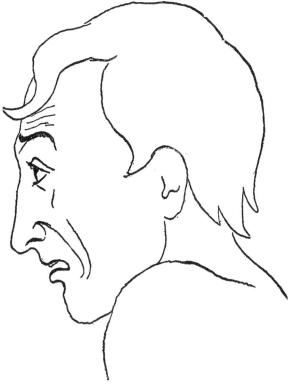

Fig. 195.

Wildness.   Sensation of a beast at bay.
Doting.

Same movements as in the last illustrations, with the difference that the head is lowered and that, instead of being petrified,
he is agitated.   Will and intelligence have departed before a
near and horrid peril, and the perturbed being, bereft of reason,
and now moved by a purely instinctive impulse, rages without
a target, and keeps turning in a circle, incapable of doing anything useful for his preservation.

Fig. 196.

Silence.

Principal movements: Head carried forward; first finger laid on pursed-up lips; eyebrows raised. This face expresses with great energy the command not to speak, the order to keep silent. Evidently the one making this sign imposes his will. Now, at first it would seem difficult to explain the connection with the elevation of the eyebrows which has always been cited as indicating absence of will, so this solution is offered: To render the command more effectual a threat accompanies it. So the expression means: Silence! on pain of something fearful! And this something fearful is definitely expressed by the raised eyebrows which always indicate fright.

All has not been said. Many omissions the author is well aware of, and perhaps some mistakes, have slipped in. Still, this would appear to be the right path, and in thus letting the reader assist in the attempt, and in disclosing this method of research, in working, as it were, under his eyes, it would seem that the student has been taught not only to follow and share the joy of the little discoveries made, but to go on further and to bring to greater perfection this first study of the Art of Pantomime, or, if preferred, this attempt to reconstruct the language of Nature.

PANTOMIME IN THE THEATER

CHAPTER I

The first part of this book has demonstrated that in all work dealing with the representation of humanity, every artist is forced to resort to the language of Nature.

Thus it would seem, if there is to be an art of acting, that this art must be cultivated, taught and guided into a path of progress leading it towards perfection.

The best way to perfect dramatic art is to play pantomimes; no longer according to individual fancy, as has been the custom, but under a system governed by certain laws, and noting the improvement gained. This is the first benefit of pantomimes.

The question may arise, does pantomime possess sufficient resources to make a show complete, intelligible, and interesting enough to offer to the public?

Many persons profess a deep disdain for pantomime and condemn it without investigation. If it is judged only from some of the examples to be seen on all sides, severe criticism is not far wrong. Most of the time the representations are of pieces poorly composed, played by actors who understand nothing of the art of dumb show, from which a natural feeling of boredom and weariness results. But neither is an ill-written play, interpreted by poor actors, a very pleasing performance.

So when it is asked if pantomime can become a spectacle worthy of the public's interest, it must be understood that this result is expected when authors and actors shall have learned the art of registering emotion properly.

Admitting that some day perfectly definite and intelligible pantomimes will be presented, it is further argued:

Will not the field of their action be very narrow?

Why have pantomime when we have drama?

Why have dumb show, when we have speech?

Why accept less, when we have the whole?

To the above questions, these answers are offered:

The first step in forming a clear opinion on pantomime is definitely to appraise its resources and its difficulties. Analysis of the fascinating elements of the eternal charm which draws the crowd to the theater includes them all in the following list:

1. The literary beauties of the play.
2. Declamation, song, and the charm of the human voice.
3. The interest due to plot and situation.
4. The stage pictures. (Movements, groups, tableaux.)
5. The acting of the artists. (Attitudes, play of features, gestures.)
6. The personality of the artists.
7. Costumes.
8. Scenery and properties.
9. Lighting effects.
10. Music.
11. Dancing.
12. Even the interest in the audience attending the show.

Is it not evident that with the exception of the first two, pantomime includes all the others?

And is it not these others that produce the captivating illusion which we seek in a performance?

In other words, is it not what a deaf person would enjoy in seeing " The Barber of Seville " played, for instance?

Or can the feelings of a blind man at the same performance be imagined? Each of these unfortunates would experience a different joy: the first would see a pantomime played; the second hear a great work rendered. It is not necessary to decide which one would lose the most.

The effort is made to show, that in all theatrical productions, pantomime occupies a large place. It is apparent that if any of these regular plays had been composed especially to be acted in dumb show and if appropriate music had been written to give emphasis to gesture and to replace speech, quite as interesting a performance might have resulted.

Understand that masterpieces are not under discussion. Appreciation for literature prevents the idea of establishing any parallel between a work of genuine literary merit, and a pantomime. It is agreed that there are works so exquisite and so sublime — such as certain dramas of de Musset or Hugo, that they gain by being studied at home without the fascinating accessories of the theater. Only the ordinary theater is under consideration, the theater for the people, the melodrama, the common vaudeville where only essential words are said, where the action is swift. And masters of characterization know well the formula: Few lines, but action, action, action. Now pantomime means putting these principles in practice to the bitter end. No words at all, nothing but action.

On the other hand, pantomime must not be regarded as a clever trick which consists in presenting a play while omitting the help of speech voluntarily and without reason; this would be absurd. This would be as childish, as useless as to attempt a literary work while omitting the use of words containing an I or an O; or to play the violin behind one's back. The difficulties of the methods employed add nothing to the literary work, nor to the playing of the violin. Generally the results are worse.

Also the public must not be asked to take into consideration the difficulties which a work in dumb show entails, but simply to consider this work from the viewpoint of the absolutely peculiar sensation which it should produce in the spectator.

Really, the principal motive for producing a pantomime is that its rapid and noiseless action causes a very different emotion than the drama does, a mysterious emotion, akin to that experienced in dreams. A painting does not speak; statues are silent; yet no one denies the intense charm which pictures and sculpture exert.

Therefore, pantomimes shall be animated pictures, our characters living statues. From every point of view these productions shall be entirely different from plays. And what matter the means, if you gain a new thrill!

"Pantomime," said Marmontel, "speaks to the eyes a more powerful language than that of words. It is even more impassioned than eloquence, and no speech can equal its warmth and force."

Doubtless in the present complex state of civilization, pantomime is unable to express all our ideas; but as Marmontel says, it expresses with greater force and passion than speech the things that belong to its field. For this reason: in the last analysis speech is a purely conventional means adopted by human beings to exchange thoughts. No word is the exclusive, necessary expression of an idea — it is only the arbitrary, conventional, accepted sign of it.

The meaning of words in use must be learned, and when they are pronounced it is by virtue of a quick effort of memory that connection is established between the symbol and the object signified, between the word and the thing.

The proof of this is that our next-door neighbors, Germans, Italians, etc., use different words to express: I love, I am hungry. So it is not surprising that a feeling expressed in words should lose some of its warmth and its power over our sensibilities in passing through this intermediary, however admirable.

Pantomime, on the contrary, speaks a language quick, spontaneous, and common to all: it is not only the accepted symbol of a sensation, it is that sensation itself. And that is why this language is not only understood, but felt.

A last argument: Readers know that verbs are the life and soul of a language and it will be demonstrated that nearly all words interpreted by mimicry are either verbs or may be turned into them. Therefore dramatic actions are living verbs, words animated, visible, active.

So it is affirmed that pantomime should be cultivated and encouraged for two reasons:

First, because it is the best means of bringing dramatic art to perfection.

Second, because it offers a performance capable of making the spectator experience an absolutely unique artistic sensation.

The sole problem for authors and artists is to learn to use the language of emotion without speech.

CHAPTER II

HOW TO REGISTER THE PARTS OF SPEECH

To make a pantomime, an author is obliged not only to write a good scenario, but also to build a play with such craftsmanship that each scene may be easily interpreted by action without words.

Moreover, he must be capable of planning the stage-setting of his play. This is impossible without a thorough knowledge of the art of acting, and the craft of the theater. In a word, he must know accurately the resources under his control and the difficulties he will meet, so as to use the former and escape the latter.

Hence the necessity for the following analysis, though the care may appear meticulous, of:

1st — What the parts of speech become when translated into the language of pantomime.

2nd — What are the dangers to avoid?

3rd — What assistance is secured by the use of stagecraft?

PRONOUNS

Personal pronouns are easily expressed by means of a simple indicative gesture.

I.	You.	He.
Me.	We.	They.

Note always that personal pronouns of the third person may only be expressed when they apply to people present.

Possessive pronouns may be expressed with equal ease.

My.	Your.	His.
Our.	Their.	Hers.

The preceding rule about the third person applies here. Demonstrative pronouns are even better expressed.

This.	These.	The latter.
That.	Those.	The former.

But relative pronouns must be entirely eliminated.

Who.   What.   Which.

As well as the following indefinite pronouns:

Others.   Such.   Whoever.   Some.

It is because of their vague and indefinite meaning that they cannot be rendered, as dramatic action is an exact language, one might say, or rather material, as it speaks only of the visible.

Some indefinite pronouns can be expressed by action when the persons or objects they refer to are present, such as:

One.	Each.	No one.
The other.	Several.	None.

In short, pronouns are not difficult.

VERBS

Levizac says: " The function of verbs is to express actions, feelings and situations."

Thus it is the greatest, and almost the only word in dramatic action, since pantomime expresses itself entirely through movement and action.

An important point about verbs is this truth stated by all grammarians: *There is only one verb, namely: to be.*

" The essential and distinctive character of verbs," Estarac says, " is to express the intellectual existence of a subject with certain modifications."

" The wish to shorten speech has led men to invent words

which include both the verb *to be* and the attribute.   He loves,
signifies: he is loving." Napoleon Landais.

It would be helpful if authors and actors would regard the
personal pronouns when gesticulated,

      I.   He.   We.   You.   They.

as signifying

      I am.   He is.   We are, etc.

which is their real meaning, as they express themselves by actually indicating the person.

      I — who am here actually present.
      You — who are there actually present.

So that when we register:

      I wish.   He sleeps.   We listen.   You weep.

the two gestures made signify expressly:

      I am — wishing.   We are — listening.
      He is — sleeping.   You are — weeping.

These examples give us only the present tense of the verb
" to be " with the present participle of to sleep, to weep, etc.
So the serious question arises: Can we conjugate verbs in all
tenses by the art of pantomime?   Evidently they cannot be con-
jugated in the exact sense of the word.   It is impossible to give
to gestures registering " you are drinking " a variation that
would indicate " you were drinking, you drank, you will drink,"
but it is possible to cause the suggestion of these periods, at
least the most important, by means of certain combinations,
on the stage, and that is the essential thing.

Take this scene, for instance:

A gentleman dressed for a ball returns home and his wife
meets him with this remark:

" While you were dancing there I was weeping here alone."

The pantomimist could act it out thus:

Out there — you dance — alone — here — I weep.

This sentence sounds very different from the first when spoken, but it is not a matter of hearing it, but of seeing it acted out. Let us examine the impression it makes.

We see a gentleman arriving from a ball. The action has taken place. This gentleman *has been* to a ball in the past. With an air of reproach, his wife says to him: " Out there — you dance." We do not hear these words, we see the gestures — the gesture " out there " signifies for us — the ball where her husband was. The gesture for " you dance " does not at all give us the idea that the gentleman actually *is dancing* but that " he was dancing out there, at the ball from which he came."

At once the spectators understand the words: " Out there — you dance " as meaning, without the least ambiguity " out there, you were dancing." And when the actress adds " Alone — here — I weep " as the spectator sees only the gestures expressing " Alone — here — I — " action of weeping, he inevitably makes the action of weeping coincide with the period of time when the gentleman was dancing.

So, for the whole, the aforesaid gestures give the sensation of the phrase: " While you were dancing out there, at the ball, alone, here, I was weeping."

" While " is a word impossible to act, but the whole of the phrase suggests it to the mind as clearly as if it were spoken.

By a slight change of scene the future may be as easily indicated as the past. Let us suppose that the gentleman, dressed for the ball, is preparing to go out. His wife detains him and makes exactly the same gestures as in the preceding case, that is:

Out — there — you dance — alone — here — I weep.

By the single fact that the gentleman is about to go out, that he is going to a ball, that he is not yet there, and therefore, he can only accomplish the action of dancing in the future, the action of the wife translates itself in the mind by the phrase: "While, out there, at the ball, you will dance; alone here, I shall weep."

And always by the same craft the suggestion of the conditional tense may be put across. If our gentleman, instead of having decided to leave, seems to hesitate, if his wife seems to feel some hope of detaining him, the sense of our phrase will naturally fall into the conditional form, thus: If you should go, out there, to the ball to dance; alone here, I should weep.

Thus it is the whole situation on the stage which naturally relates the acted verb to the time desired.

The actor's only concern is to learn the different types of movements which must be executed to express clearly the meaning of each verb. Studied from this viewpoint, verbs acted out can be divided into two distinct classes:

1 — Verbs signifying action.
2 — Verbs signifying feeling.

Verbs of action are those expressed by the dumb show of simulating an act. Notice that they are expressed by voluntary, studied, constructed movements. Also notice that they are expressed principally by gestures, properly so called, that is: with the hands, the arms, the legs.

| To read. | To sew. | To call. |
| To write. | To scan. | To push away. |

are verbs of action.

Verbs signifying sensation include all verbs expressed by imitating the signs which betray an emotion or a feeling. These are distinguished from verbs of action because the movements expressing them are involuntary, instinctive, spontaneous. These are especially portrayed by facial expression, such as:

| To tremble. | To be astonished. | To fear. |
| To admire. | To laugh. | To weep. |

The possibility of expressing them depends, as do all other words, on the greater or less obviousness of the signs or actions which characterize either the action or feeling. Thus it is evident that the verbs:

| To combine. | To philosophize. | To compute. |
| To multiply. | To be patient. | To persevere. |

offer infinitely more difficulties than the verbs:

| To drink. | To be astonished. | To call, etc. |

Articles of speech cannot be dramatized, but as in many spoken languages, the language of acting can do very well without them.

How to Interpret Nouns

In pantomime, no nouns exist because it is impossible to portray a single one by acting. At first this statement will surprise many people and especially actors. To convince yourself of this fact attempt to translate by dumb show the simplest nouns, for instance:

| A fan. | A beggar. |

In vain you will try to describe by gestures or to outline in space the shape of a fan, the profile of a beggar. You will be forced in despair to the only possible means, which is — to make the gesture of fanning yourself, to express the word fan; to make the gesture of asking alms to express the word beggar. For all the world knows that one fans oneself with a fan, and that a man who solicits help is a beggar.

Neither can it be denied, that after having said " Give me," if the gesture of fanning oneself is added, everyone will understand that a fan is asked for.

But it is no less true that the actor has not said: " Give me a fan," but really " Give me what is used to fan oneself." Now the verb *to fan* is not the noun *fan,* but that is what happens to all nouns, without exception.

Notice further that in the majority of cases the nouns will not be expressed by the verbs from which they grew, as *fan* grew from *to fan,* but often by verbs which will not, as words, have any connection with these nouns.

Thus a key will be indicated by the verb to open. " Give me the key " will be translated as " Give me what is used to open " (what will serve, being understood).

In short, the noun key becomes the verb to open.

Here are some names of objects and the verbs which characterize their functions:

A pen (what is used)	To write.
A comb (what is used)	To comb one's hair.
A glass (what is used)	To drink.
A needle (what is used)	To sew.

People and animals are indicated by the verb which describes their habitual action, or their function, or their manner of living.

A coachman (whose habitual action is) To drive.

A sweeper (whose habitual action is) To sweep.

A leader of an orchestra (whose habitual action is) To beat the time.

A swordsman (whose habitual action is) To defend himself.

A dog (whose habitual action is) To bark.

A horse (whose habitual action is) To gallop.

Qualities are rendered by the impression they make on us.

Beauty (moves us)	To admire.
Ridicule (moves us)	To jeer.
Scandal (moves us)	To exclaim.
Danger (moves us)	To be afraid.
The unexpected (moves us)	To be astonished.
Modesty (moves us)	To drop the eyes.
Hypocrisy (moves us)	To dissemble.
Self-conceit (moves us)	To carry the head high.
Rapacity (moves us)	To steal, to clutch.

Very many nouns can only be indicated by one or several verbs which characterize the habit or the action of another object which, nevertheless, is appropriate to suggest the idea of the noun that cannot be directly expressed.

For example: a boat, that which is used in the action of rowing (in using oars). Thus the noun boat is suggested by the verb to row (to use oars).

There are some nouns which no verb can express, nor even suggest the custom, the action, or the way of living, like:

A citizen.   An employee.   A month.   A virtue.   A turnip. and all proper names. These cause the most difficulty.

How to Act Adjectives

The following division of adjectives into four special classes has no connection with rules of grammar.

1. Adjectives derived from verbs are considered as verbs.
2. Adjectives of imitation are summed up in verbs of action.
3. Adjectives of sensation are summed up in verbs of feeling.
4. Adjectives of description can be expressed by a gesture.

Thus, except for the fourth class, which contains a very small number of words, all adjectives in pantomime must be treated as verbs, or expressed by verbs. The first category, those derived from verbs and considered only as verbs; such as:

Smiling women.   Dancing women.   Jumping women. are women putting into action the verbs — to smile — to dance — to jump.

The second class of imitative adjectives which resolve themselves into verbs signifying action must be expressed by the imitation of the action which characterizes a permanent quality or an accidental state.

Lively is rendered as	To move quickly.
Lazy is rendered as	To walk with indolence.
Happy is rendered as	To smile, to expand, or beam.
Unhappy is rendered as	To suffer, to be sad.
Cowardly is rendered as	One who trembles.
Courageous is rendered as	One who defies, who faces.
Obsequious is rendered as	One who bows, who is eager.

Adjectives of sensation resolve themselves into verbs signifying sensation and are expressed by the signs of the impressions their quality produces on a person.

Sweet, sugared (which makes the impression of) pleasing the lips.

Perfumed (which makes the impression of) dilating the nostrils.

Beautiful (which makes the impression of) rejoicing the eyes.

Amiable (which makes the impression of) attracting.

Drunken (which makes the impression of) upsetting the mind.

Shocking (which makes the impression of) repulsing.

Descriptive adjectives are those whose quality, shape, size or quantity may be described by gestures.

One.	Small.	Flat.
Five.	Thin.	Folded.
First.	Long.	Stooped.
Second.	Round.	Blind of one eye.
Tall.	Pointed.	One-armed.

There are some adjectives whose quality can only be expressed by similitude, that is, by pointing out a visible object, other than the one spoken of, but which ostensibly possesses the special quality that is meant; thus:

Blue.	Gilded.	Hard.
Yellow.	Polished.	Soft.
Red.	Varnished.	Dry.

This manner of expressing adjectives is a very delicate art. Finally there will be encountered a considerable number of adjectives which cannot be rendered by any of these methods; all such as contain an abstract idea, for instance:

Useful.	Ephemeral.
Indispensable.	Incessant.
Simple.	Approximate.
Complicated.	Scientific.
Administrative.	Philosophical.
Provisional.	Symbolic.

How to Render Adverbs

In the first place all adverbs ending in *ly* and formed of a preposition and noun, like sadly, joyously, which, analyzed, mean with sadness, with joy, are not considered. They will simply be turned into nouns and treated as such, which means they will become the verbs to suffer, to rejoice, etc.

Adverbs of Location

Where.	Above.	To the left.	Within.
Here.	Below.	Before.	Without.
There.	To the right.	Behind.	Opposite.

Negative and Affirmative Adverbs

Certainly.	Always.	No.
Yes.		Never.

Doubtful Adverbs

Perhaps.	Probably.	Possibly.

Question Adverbs

When?	How many?	How?

These words present no difficulty, except that the word "always" could not be expressed clearly.

Adverbs of Sequence

First.	Last.	Confusedly.
In file.	In front.	Together.

ADVERBS OF QUANTITY

How many?	Much.	Hardly any.
Few.	More.	Enough.

These words may be easily expressed by dramatic art.

ADVERBS OF MANNER

Well.	Very well.	Badly.
Very badly.	Gropingly.	Behind.
On the other side.	Backward.	Accidentally.

This group comprises about fifty very expressive words which may be interpreted quite conveniently.

COMPARATIVE ADVERBS

Separately.	Better and better.	Above all.
Worse and worse.	Apart.	Aside.

Neither do these present impossibilities.

To sum up, these adverbs in constant use do not present difficulties which may not be overcome. Unfortunately the following group of exceedingly important words cannot be expressed in dumb show.

ADVERBS OF TIME

At present.	Suddenly.	Yesterday.	Soon.
Tomorrow.	Ordinarily.	The past.	Today.
Henceforth.	Too soon.	Sometimes.	Otherwise.
But just now.	Long while.	Suddenly.	Rarely.
Before.	After tomorrow.	Early.	Late.
After.	In the future.	Too late.	Not yet.
Before yesterday.	Right now.	Then.	All at once.

The impossibility of expressing these adverbs is caused by the lack of any visible sign able to interpret ideas of time, of duration, of succession, of precedence, etc. In pantomime the actor would be forced to fall back on almanacs or calendars, in short, on inscriptions.

PREPOSITIONS

A single group contains about twenty words:

According to.	As.	Besides.
By.	For want of.	By the means.
Except.	At least.	In regard to.
In regard to.	In place of.	At the cost of.
In spite of.	As far as.	Because of.
Regarding.	Without.	Because.

The translation of these words into gestures must also be given up. But they are less to be regretted than adverbs of time, and the action of the pantomime can omit them without inconvenience.

CONJUNCTIONS

Here are about thirty of these words:

And.	For.	But.
Because.	In consequence.	Besides.
That is to say.	Although.	Since.
Nevertheless.	As soon as.	Or.
Provided that.	After all.	Thus.
At last.	Also.	Meanwhile.
Since.	Then.	Always.
At least.	That's why.	At last.
During.	Whether.	
In order to.	Pertinent.	

These words offer the same difficulties as the preceding groups. But, as a matter of fact, though these words inject clearness and precision into conversation, many of them merely gratify the ear. They are unnecessary in pantomime.

INTERJECTIONS

As interjections when spoken are usually accompanied by violent gesticulations, the feeling at least can be given by imitating these movements.

To SUM UP:

Pronouns can be easily expressed.   Remember that personal pronouns take the meaning of the verb " to be."

Verbs are the life and wealth of pantomime.   Remember that the past and future tenses are indicated by the combination of situations on the stage.

Nouns no longer exist, they are all turned into verbs.

Adjectives, except for a small number indicating quantity, shape or size, are turned into verbs.

Adverbs ending in *ly* become verbs by analysis.   There are about one hundred and fifty others which can be interpreted without great difficulty, except adverbs of time which are completely beyond the powers of pantomime, a fact much to be regretted.

Interjections convey their sensations by imitation of the gestures that usually accompany them.

Articles, Prepositions, Conjunctions cannot be rendered by the actor's art.   But their meaning is readily understood by the spectator so that their lack need not be deplored.

In short, with comparatively few exceptions, all the words that can be expressed by dumb show are, or can be forced to become, *verbs.*

CHAPTER III

PROBLEMS OF THE SILENT DRAMA

There was no intention of compiling a list of words to be employed and a list of words to be rejected. It is enough to point out the way to recognize them.

Let us list again the five kinds of dramatic movements, given earlier in this volume.

1st. Character Movements: — whose purpose is to build up permanent attitudes which portray a character, its quality, mood, age, importance, etc.

2nd. Action Movements: — which are those actually necessary to accomplish a definite action.

3rd. Sensation Movements: — which are the signs by which all emotions are involuntarily betrayed.

4th. Complementary Movements: — which accompany a principal movement with the object of giving it greater force or obviousness, or merely make an attitude more harmonious.

These four kinds of action are necessary, spontaneous, and inevitable. Every one makes them, recognizes and comprehends them. They are basic elements of the language of Nature because Nature itself teaches them to us. They are the immediate expression of action or feeling. Thus they belong equally to actors of spoken drama as to actors in a pantomime or on the screen.

The imitation of these movements never offers great difficulty. They need only be reproduced with accuracy and truthfulness.

There is a fifth class of action called Descriptive or Speaking Movements. These differ greatly from the preceding in being intended, invented and constructed. They are not expressions of an action or of a sensation actually done or felt but only the outline of an action, the suggestion of a sensation. These movements do not signifiy that such a thing *is*, but rather that it *has been* or *will be*. They no longer show the fact, the fact itself, but solely the bringing to mind of this fact.

They have not the same claim to the title of Language of Nature as the four first classes of movements, they are already an artificial language. In short, descriptive or speaking actions aim to take the place of speech and that is why their proper sphere is restricted to silent drama. This is a very important distinction and the reader is urged to accept these divisions of the dramatic language of Nature and the dramatic language of Art.

This example will illustrate the five classes:

A character appears carrying his head high, his chest and abdomen prominent; his gesture is decided; his walk assured: these constitute *" character movements "* which reveal to the spectator the idea of a bold sport. He pours out a glass of wine and drinks it: *action movements*.

He makes a grimace of horror and disgust: *an action of sensation*.

The body is carried on the backward leg, the head is tossed back, the hands push away the glass: *complementary movements*.

Up to this point an acting and feeling character presents himself who belongs equally to drama and to pantomime. He has used only the language of Nature.

But suppose he must say: " Gracious! what vile wine! " (Indicating another bottle) " Fortunately, here is some better." In a play the actor will speak these two lines, but when a silent drama is under way, the actor will be obliged to invent the movements needed to translate rapidly and clearly the words he may not speak. Thus these movements will be an artificial language and then difficulties begin. Truly it is easy enough to register " Gracious! Vile! Fortunately, this one delicious! "

But suppose the phrase to be expressed is this: "That twists my insides!" It is still easy to imagine a satisfactory pantomime. The actor would grasp his abdomen in both hands and his face would express pain, then he would energetically act out the verb to twist as if he were wringing a cloth. This is more complicated, but still quite clear. He would simply have replaced the word "insides" by the word "abdomen."

But if he ought to say: "That's like velvet." If he should have no velvet on his costume nor in reach of his hand, he will face an embarrassing problem.

He will have to be satisfied by gently stroking his throat with his fingers, assume an air of bliss, and the line will be replaced by: "Soft to the throat."

If any velvet is within reach, he will caress it with his finger tips and the line will be translated: "Soft to my throat as velvet is soft to my fingers." But be warned that this linking together of the sensation the wine causes in passing down the throat and the sensation which velvet conveys to the fingers is a very complicated explanation, of doubtful taste, and had better be omitted. It would thus be better to hold to the phrase "soft to the throat" without bringing in the idea of velvet.

As a general rule comparisons should not be used except when it would be impossible to make the meaning plain without their help.

Take another line: "I would prefer to drink water."

If no water was on the table this would bring the actor face to face with an absolute impossibility. In fact, apart from the verb *to drink,* he could not express the verb "prefer" any better than the noun "water."

If the actor is required to show that he prefers the wine in the second bottle to the wine in the first, nothing could be easier. But, to express in pantomime the verb "to prefer" when the object of such preference is absent is impossible. Because "to prefer" is a process of thought which can only be rendered visible by a material manifestation. Furthermore, he cannot portray the noun "water" because water does not possess form or quality sufficiently characteristic to be described and understood. Therefore writers should omit phrases which present these difficulties. It is possible to recognize such by observing the following law:

We can register through pantomime words signifying an action, a quality, a person or an object by imitation or description of the action, the feeling, the shape, the attitude, the function or the habit, with this condition: That this act, this feeling, this shape, this attitude, this function, or this habit possesses such a distinct individuality, so known and characteristic that the portrayal of this distinguishing trait will be sufficient to arouse clearly, spontaneously and without confusion in the mind of the spectator the image or idea of the act, the quality, the person or the object intended.

Examples:

To pray. The action of praying is imitated by joining the hands.

Fearful: The sensation of fear is portrayed.

An old man: The attitude of a person who walks stooped over, and leaning on a stick is imitated.

A violinist: The gesture of the habitual action is copied, which is to wield the violin bow.

A comb: The actor pretends to comb his hair, which is the use made of a comb.

The individuality which marks each of these words is quite sufficient so that the description or imitation of this particular trait shall clearly evoke the idea the action seeks to express.

Unfortunately there are a great number of words which lack this essential individuality and therefore are absolutely impossible to register by pantomime. Such as:

Lately, I was virtuous.

At present, you are a citizen.

Soon they will be employed.

Get me a way to earn my living.

When my father became a widower, he gave up his job.

My creditors are hard to deal with.

My uncle is chief of the Bureau of the Minister of Commerce.
My mother gave me an example of devotion and self-sacrifice.
Bread is expensive.
Art is difficult.
I have learned many things.
Life is a decoy.

Although very simple ideas and very familiar persons were purposely selected, here are a dozen little sentences that could never be interpreted by pantomime because none of the words composing them offer sufficiently striking characteristics.

As a matter of fact, there are no gesticulations capable of characterizing a father, a mother, an uncle, a creditor, just now, at present, soon, virtuous, citizen, widower, office, devotion, etc. Should the dramatist suppose that the majority of words are in this class he is tempted to despair and give up pantomime. But nothing must be exaggerated. In the first place, among the untranslatable lines which flow from the pen, many may be easily expressed just by changing the terms.

Besides, among the phrases that must be definitely discarded, there will be found a great number whose feeling may be given by other means than direct expression. And finally, if everything cannot be portrayed in the language of dumb show, nevertheless, many things can be so expressed, and precisely the most valuable things from the point of view of the theater. Of course, compared with the French or English tongue, pantomime is a restricted language — that is admitted. But still it is broad enough to satisfy the requirements of certain types of plays. Simply use it with ingenuity.

At any rate, it is certain that writers and actors who make a conscientious study of this work will have at their command a much richer language than the one customarily used in pantomimes and ballets. Another valuable point is, they will also have the advantage of being able to avoid the obscurity, the tedious passages, the banalities, the puzzles which usually abound in this kind of show, to such a degree that it is astonishing that they have not been entirely abandoned.

To SUM UP:

The dramatic language of Nature, which is used by the speaking actor as well as the silent, never presents difficulties.

On the other hand, the *artificial* dramatic language whose aim is to supplant speech, and which is reserved exclusively for the silent drama on screen or stage, is limited by its problems and impossibilities.

Generally speaking — and this is the weakness of pantomimes — great difficulties will be encountered as soon as action, or the dialogue of action, is abandoned and narration attempted.

The specially dangerous situations to be guarded against are:

To speak of an object not on the stage.

To speak of an absent person, or one who has not yet appeared.

To tell a past action or outline a future one.

After what has been said, it is evident that the fate of a pantomime depends above all on the author, whose foremost principles should be to avoid the dangers just indicated, and to select such situations and scenes of action that the interpreters will never be faced by an insurmountable difficulty.

CHAPTER IV

THE CHOICE OF A SUBJECT

In principle all varieties of plays are good; vaudeville, comedy, drama, farce and fantasy can all be staged as pantomimes. But just any subject must not be adopted indifferently. The difficulties of registering the silent drama suffice to explain this.

Thus it would be easier to construct a pantomime out of *George Dandin* than out of *Les Précieuses Ridicules* — out of *Don César de Basan* than Hugo's *Hernani* — out of Sardou's plays than those of Corneille, because the essence of pantomime is action, while to express thought frequently exceeds the limits of this language. Lofty moral and philosophic teaching may be extracted from a pantomime and it is capable of supporting striking ideas or a definite thesis, but on condition that the arguments be rendered by action, the demonstration be of actual facts, and that their eloquence be that of life and motion.

Forms must be given up and axioms discarded, but plot remains and putting it into action. On the field of the silent drama parade all the passions, all the sentiments, all the needs, all the desires which urge men to act and to struggle. Upon the whole, all motives which stimulate humanity and urge it into deeds can be summed up in the one Law of Conservation, — conservation of the individual and conservation of the race.

It would seem as if the whole universe, beings and things alike, obeyed the supreme command — Live. To live, to save himself, to be, in spite of all accidents, competitions, and all the dangers which assail the individual who wants his place in the sun, — and who fights to get it.

Let your stage characters exist and behave in obedience to this law. Arouse the will to possess, raise up obstacles to success, force passions to a climax, and soon, by adding details that may be infinitely varied, you will have created a drama of action keen enough to captivate and hold your audience.

Of course you cannot command all the elements which writers of plays employ. You would be unable to translate suitably the changing frivolities of manner, the latest joke, the new slang, the ephemeral kind of wit of a more or less refined and conventional society, which is the same as saying it is more or less apart from natural life. But there remain all the indefeasible natural urges of Life, and this is the essential point.

You will only be bound to arrange your scenes in such a way that each will be explained by the next, and that action shall succeed action. Your scenario should be a logical sequence of facts, the present fact giving the motive for the following. So the value of the work will depend on first, the choice of the subject, and second, the ingenuity of construction.

The loftier flights of pantomime may have been curtailed by the error common to many writers who imagine that a pantomime cannot do without Pierrot, Harlequin and Columbine, imaginary stock characters whose qualities are so defined that hardly any room is left for originality or the unforeseen.

This explains why most pantomimes have such strong resemblance to one another, both in their methods and in the impression they communicate.

It would be well to abandon these too well known types, which, moreover, we no longer know how to use to advantage. All the more as it has been urged on writers to enlarge the boundaries of the silent drama and supply their characters with more delicate and complex qualities and feelings.

The public is constantly offered Pierrots, witty, kind and poetic, with qualities and faults altogether universal; Harlequins, who walk and act like ordinary people; Columbines, who are either young leading ladies or coquettes absolutely modern in their wiles and sentiments. Now what good is a Pierrot without his stupidity, his laziness, his yearnings for the joys of the bottle and the table? What is Harlequin without his mask and wooden sword, without his pirouets and his cutting pigeon-wings in the dance? What is Columbine without her innocence, her inconsistencies, as of a fairy child?

It is not meant that this special type should be prohibited, since all types are good, as has been said, but let it be presented properly reconstructed with all its traditions, its broad fun, its blows with a club, its dances, its fairies, and its Bengal fires. The point to be avoided is to force these characters, or rather these costumes, to become parts of a pantomime where they are not necessary, where they are out of harmony, above all where they are mingled in the most uncouth way with modern characters. And really what would Harlequin and a modern flapper have to say to each other? What affinity of ideas could exist between them? So with whatever kind intentions the mind of the public is tormented by having such problems put before it there is a lack of logic and harmony which annoys the spectator and to which he cannot adjust himself.

The question may be equally put, what good is Pierrot in a modern play? Or what good is a Pierrot without his white costume? " Suppress Pierrot! " people exclaim. Is it possible? Can there be a pantomime without Pierrot? Aren't most pantomines called " Pierrot this — Pierrot that " ?

But a little reflection will convince anyone that in the pantomime which must be created in future Pierrot is useless and even inadmissible. There was a time when Pierrot was only the white-smudged servant of Cassandra the miller, a flour-covered simpleton, a secondary character. He was a blockhead, a dumb servant, lazy and starved, the only stimulants to his tricks being his desire to satisfy his appetites.

Debureau [1] first played him in this manner. But soon his genius burst through the rôle and gave birth to Pierrot, that is,

---

[1] Debureau, a celebrated French pantomimist, lived between 1796 and 1846. He created the rôle of the flour-covered Pierrot at the Little Theatre of Funambules, at Paris, where George Sand, Gautier and other notables acclaimed him as " the greatest artist of the time." He could translate the most varied sentiments by a wink of the eye, a line of the mouth, a frown of an eyebrow or a sly gesture. (Quoted from *Dictionnaire Larousse illustré*.)

to a type more full, more white, more malicious, who ended by giving more kicks than he received and holding for himself alone the sympathy and applause of the audience. So great was his success that he made the mistake of forcing people to believe the pantomime was Pierrot, and this error still prevails.

Could it be claimed that *L'Enfant Prodige,* the most successful pantomime at the beginning of the century, would have been less interesting if the rôles of Father Pierrot and Son Pierrot had been played in the natural colors of the face? Indeed it could not.

L'Enfant Prodige is one of the most true to life of realistic comedies and could only gain by preserving in all its details the appearances of the strictest naturalness. Has the face of an actor a greater power of expression when it is whitened? To believe that is another error. The whiteness of the face causes the teeth and eyeballs to appear a dull gray, thus dimming the brightness of the smile, and the brightness of the glance. This peculiar use of white draws attention to an actor and distinguishes him from the rest of the cast, but the drama without words is not the gainer by it, quite the contrary. In the first place, if this white coating was so useful a means all the characters in a pantomime would hasten to adopt it. At least this would give the spectator the relief of no longer being shocked when a being with white skin performs among people with pink skins, without the latter showing any surprise. This coating of white grease paint could take the place of the antique mask with the advantage of not depriving the actor of the play of his features. Yet it would remain a mask, which is bad in principle.

The face of the miller's servant accidentally covered with flour had a natural cause, the unexplained whiteness of Pierrot has none. It is no less absurd to make up children white. In short, writers are urged to put aside these characters of ancient pantomime, including that of Pierrot himself.

Does not real life provide interesting rôles in abundance? Is it not full of curious types and queer people, capable of amusing and stirring the spectator? Simply select those of most strongly marked characteristics, so that from the moment of their entrance their business will be recognized. In all cases it is the author's duty to present them in so clear a fashion that no confusion is possible.

That great problem in all dramatic works, the exposition of preceding conditions, is more difficult in pantomime since it can only be told by visible means. The scenery will show the place of the action, the costumes will indicate the period, and also the rank of characters. The *heads* of the actors will furnish valuable information about their age, temperament and characteristics, and finally the stage properties will serve as a dictionary, if it may be so expressed.

The state of mind of the characters should be clearly ascertained from the very first acts they perform. As soon as a character enters, the audience must know who he is and what he wants. If it is the lover, let him try to see his mistress, even by risking the greatest adventures; if the lady, or the girl, requites his feeling let her at once perpetrate some imprudent act; if it is a jealous husband let him appear with all the signs of a man preyed upon by the most horrible suspicions; if a marriage is to take place, adorn the scene with all the paraphernalia of a wedding. In short, instruct the audience, no matter how, but immediately, in all it is indispensable for it to know. This is of such importance that the awkwardness of the business used will be easily pardoned provided it is clear. This arranged, the writer can draw a long breath, turn his attention to details later, study and develop the characters, shade the intrigues of the plot, and let the climax burst out when in his judgment the right moment has arrived, for he will have secured the interest of the spectator.

Then it will only be necessary to lay out the scenes in the order most propitious to make them understandable. For this point must be insisted on, an identical piece of stage business may prove very easy, or impossible to act out in dumb show, according to the way the writer makes his puppets move — how they make their entrances — and whether they meet before a certain time or later — and whether a certain scene is enacted before a certain other.

The best pantomimes will be composed of scenes which would each when considered by itself gain in power by being acted out silently even if it occurred in a play. Here is one example among thousands: In *Frou-Frou*, when the wronged husband, having discovered the retreat of the fugitive lovers, comes into his wife's presence he is so overwhelmed with emotion that he is about to faint; a glass of water is offered him, he stretches out his arm, but suddenly remembering the place he is in, he pulls himself together by a powerful effort of will and pushes away the glass. At each performance the public applauded this scene, where not a word was spoken.

CHAPTER V

HOW TO WRITE A PANTOMIME

The scenario of a pantomime is the same as the scenario of any kind of a play. It requires the same qualities of composition; an interesting idea, as many new situations as possible, great order in the continuity of scenes, management of the suspense and the big effects; finally, an ingenious dénouement, as all the world knows. Nearly all scenarios possess some of these qualities. At first they are only outlines, for a scenario is neither a ballet, nor a pantomime, nor a drama, nor an opera. It may become one or the other of these works, but it is yet only the germ of becoming such a work.

When a scenario has pleased a director, then the author, according to the theater where he hopes it will be produced, forces himself to compose the vaudeville sketch, or the comedy, or the opera he has in mind. He never harbors the notion that his scenario is the piece itself and that he need not write it out. Then why should authors imagine they have completed their work when they have written only the scenario of a ballet or a pantomime?

In a pantomime picked up at hazard, entitled, " The Statue," by Paul Arene, it says:

" Scarcely has Cassandra departed when Pierrot runs up. He plants a kiss on the tips of Columbine's fingers and leads her gallantly to a grassy knoll. There by the light of the moon ensues a *very lively dialogue*."

Further on Harlequin sits beside Columbine and " begins to woo her."

In " Heart of Gold Pierrot," by Lucien Cressonnois and Abel Mercklein, it is written:

"*An animated conversation* is established between the butterfly and Pierrot," and again:

"Pierrot has wits, he finds the happy phrase."

It is not necessary to multiply such instances. All librettos of pantomime are written in this manner and to most directors appear quite finished.

But this is what happens on the day of the first rehearsal. The love scene is to be rehearsed; the musician has found a charming melody; it is tender, pleasing and original. During three minutes everyone shows delight. The composer is congratulated on his happy inspiration.

But what of the actors now? Harlequin and Columbine consult their book, and find this:

"Harlequin sits beside Columbine and begins to woo her."
Or:

"An animated conversation ensues between Harlequin and Columbine." And:

"Harlequin has wits, he finds the happy phrase."

The two artists look at each other with embarrassment, they are full of good intentions, besides, they are well-known actors of talent and experience; and now they are completely nonplussed, their faces express distraction, sweat forms on their foreheads. Everyone is surprised, the musician halts.

"Repeat it." He shouts to the actors,

"We are at the 'animated conversation.'"

In his turn the author or the stage manager starts to speak:

"What ails you, looking at each other like two mummies? Put some pep into it. — You are young and beautiful and adore one another, you have only to say it to each other to prove it, it's simple enough. Once more."

They begin again; the unhappy actors outline some vague gestures; begin to cut a figure; then stop again, much worried by feeling themselves perfectly ridiculous. Around them people begin to murmur disagreeable comments. The musical director is uneasy, the author vexed.

" The actors," he says, " should at least know their trade, these will spoil my piece."

The artists make apologies, they too imagine they have done wrong, while what they ought to reply to the author is:

" We are told here to act out a lively dialogue, but where is the dialogue? What remarks shall we make? What thoughts exchange? Did you take the pains to write them? No. Have you authorized us to compose ourselves this scene which exists nowhere? No, indeed. Then what do you want us to act? Having nothing to express we express nothing, which is quite natural. So take back your scenario and make a play out of it, and we will do our best to interpret it."

Either through ignorance or timidity actors never do object in this fashion. Nevertheless, the author begins to suspect dimly that his famous script is not as perfect as he believed.

Of course, the best way would be to interrupt the rehearsals and go write the missing scenes, but an author will never confess that he has just perceived that he was wrong in bringing an incomplete work, and besides, is not this the customary way of planning all pantomimes?

In such a case this is what always happens:

" What bothers you? " the author demands of Harlequin. " What you have to do is easy, you are Columbine's lover, you take her hand — good —, you draw her to the grassy seat — very good. Columbine drops her eyes — charming. You tell her that you love her."

(Here the actor given the rôle of Harlequin puts his hands on his heart and moves his shoulders.)

Then the author cries,

" That's it! very good! perfect! "

As there is still much music to be played, Columbine again begins to drop her eyes, Harlequin continues to move his shoulders. Perhaps he will develop enough originality to add stock gestures signifying, " Your face is pretty," and the author will repeat, —

" That's it! very good! perfect! "

Very good? No. It is not perfect. This dialogue is neither lively nor new. It is not even a dialogue, it is simply the peak of the trite, the commonplace.

The public has seen this phantom of a scene, precisely as null and void, in a hundred pantomimes preceding this, and will still see it in thousands more unless writers decide actually to compose the conversations announced in their sketches instead of being satisfied to write, " Here an animated conversation takes place."

For all these types of directions, such as:

" A violent discussion arises between — " etc.

" With passionate eloquence, Pierrot persuades — "

" After exhausting all arguments — Pierrot is clever —, he finds happy lines."

All these sentences mean absolutely nothing except, " Here there is a hiatus in my pantomime," and in many manuscripts submitted there is little besides the hiatus.

Writers would never allow themselves to make similar omissions in a play. Let them realize that they are just as important in a pantomime. Probably they are unconsciously influenced by the idea that since the mummers do not speak, what use to write a dialogue for them? No, they do not speak, but they act, they do not express themselves in words, but they express themselves in the language of the drama, always provided that they have something to express.

If a scene is given them written like a play they may not succeed in translating every bit, perhaps, but at least they will interpret a good deal and that will be much more than nothing. When the writer shall acquire sufficient knowledge of the art of pantomime to know that certain phrases are actable and others are not, he will write his dialogue accordingly, and the actor will only have to translate his thought.

Then the lovers will no longer be content to place their hands on their hearts and wiggle their shoulders; they will play a scene as it was conceived. There will no longer be seen in such silent dramas the gestures and attitudes whose hackneyed dullness ends by boring the warmest partisan of pantomimes. Such a writer will truly make an original play and will be astonished himself at the eloquence of this mute language whose resources are little suspected.

Another question arises here. What style of writing should be used in these dialogues? It is easy to understand that it would be only useless trouble and even a hindrance to adorn the manuscript with witty words, phrases not yet standardized, new qualifications, and delicate effects of sonority which shape a line beautifully. That does not mean there can be no wit in the dramatic language. According to the situation a gesture may show a malicious purpose, a double-meaning, or a subtle allusion. But the interest must be in the idea and not the form. The writer must remember; — " *The literary lines should be only the means of making the actor understand his thought.*" So the best style will be the simplest, the clearest, and the most precise.

Moreover, as will soon be described, the dialogue should undergo a first translation to adapt it strictly to expression in dumb show. So the way to write a pantomime is exactly the same as that used to write a play, with the sole difference that the author is bound to avoid lines which cannot be interpreted by action, and that he should give attention to stage directions.

CHAPTER VI

HOW TO TRANSLATE IT

The words of a written line are the author's only means of explaining his thought to the interpreters. It does not follow that the acting must scrupulously express every word; more often the action will interpret better the idea of the phrase by modifying it somewhat. To translate a literary line into the language of dramatic action consists in;

First; — Reducing it to the special words that can be adequately acted out.

Second; — Deciding on the sequence these words should follow.

For the first example, the phrase already used when discussing the verb, will be repeated.

" While you were dancing at the ball, alone here, I was weeping."

For the actor this line will be reduced to the words, —

" You — out there — dance — alone — here — I weep."

Notice that this line is translated nearly word for word just because of its lack of superfluity, which brings it very close to dramatic language. Another example; —

" When everyone is asleep, come down to meet me here, I beg you."

Translation, —

" To the right — to the left — all asleep — you — from above — come down — here — I pray."

Here is another; —

" Alas! She will not come. What I heard was the beating of my heart."

Which is thus turned, —

" Alas — she — here — no. I — hear — my — heart — beat."

These examples are all easy. The acting translation differs little from the text.

But frequently difficulties are encountered which compel the adapter to modify expressions noticeably, either by equivalents or close similarities, while always respecting the meaning. Take the phrase of Tartufe; —

" Cover this bosom so I shall not see it. By such objects souls are wounded. And they bring wicked thoughts."

At first sight it seems a troublesome problem, especially the last two lines which present an idea in abstract form. Therefore the thought must be made concrete and the selection modified thus; —

" Cover this bosom from which I turn away my eyes.
Such objects scandalize me.
They arouse desires in me which cause me horror."

Translation for acting —

" Cover — your bosom — my eyes turn away — my hands push back. — These objects — me — scandalize.

" They — me — desire — move my feelings — repel with horror."

In spite of the changes forced upon the passage this dramatic translation will render quite closely the idea of the spoken words. This instance should encourage authors of pantomime to have no fear in developing their dialogue as far as appears to them necessary.

Of course all Molière's comedies could not be translated, and, moreover, they were not made to be mimed. The aim was to prove that it is possible to express by pantomime much more complicated sentences and scenes than is generally believed. It is sufficient to choose the correct figures and terms to facilitate its interpretation.

Of course there are phrases which must be cut out. Nevertheless, this is no reason to completely abandon the hope of expressing an idea. In the majority of cases a combination will be discovered which will render it, if not in entirety, at least partially.

Beaumarchais furnishes an example of a phrase absolutely impossible to register silently in " Barber of Seville," Act I, Scene II:

Figaro: " Considering the virtues required of a servant, is your Excellency acquainted with many masters who are worthy of being valets? "

Not only is this sentence in an abstract form, but also the words composing it cannot be acted out. But supposing that Figaro had come to offer himself to the Count as a servant, suppose also, that he was known to have certain faults, and that the Count, displaying a livery, said to him,

" Go away. You are not worthy of wearing that." (That is, to become his servant.)

Then the following scene may be imagined:

Figaro; — " You play cards? "

Count; — " Yes."

Figaro; — " You like pretty girls? "

Count; — " Of course."

Figaro; — " Occasionally you drink to the point where your mind is disturbed? "

Count; — " I confess it."

Figaro; — (Imitating the Count's gestures) " Go to. Neither are you worthy of wearing that livery."

It is apparent that this little scene lacks the qualities of the sentence to be translated, but it is no less true that the excessive exactions of masters have been expressed, either well or ill, and that is the author's idea. Such changes may seem a kind of sacrilege when a work of Molière or Beaumarchais is under consideration, but they are perfectly legitimate when practiced on ordinary manuscripts. That is the kind of operation to which all scenes containing dialogue must be submitted.

This preliminary work offers valuable benefits. First, a script nearly freed from untranslatable phrases; definite information for the stage manager; an astonishing rapidity in getting up a show, and great confidence and eagerness on the part of the cast. In short, a better pantomime, and better acted.

CHAPTER VII

THE USE OF THEATRICAL ACCESSORIES

SCENERY

An author should demand that this be as correct as possible, and need not fear to overload it with any details capable of defining the place and the epoch.

WRITINGS ON THE STAGE

Inscriptions on walls, signs on shops, notices of sale, signposts of location, hand-bills and tickets, are all devices that can be of great service, and even if their presence be a little forced, no one will criticize their use.

PROPERTIES

Properties play a much more important part in a pantomime than in a drama. To such a degree are they indispensable that the director is advised even to infringe the law of probability to introduce necessary objects on the stage, though it would not be natural to find them in the settings.

Suppose, for instance, an actor is given this line to mime; —
" I have just consulted my barometer, it reads . . . "

The one in this rôle might be quite puzzled, for to attempt to delineate a barometer would be hopeless. Must the line then be cut out? Supposing it was absolutely essential to consult a barometer? What should the author do? Replace the line: " I have just consulted my barometer," by this: " The actor consults the barometer."

If the scene is set in a parlor or study it would be quite natural to hang a barometer there, and the actor, instead of being faced by an impossibility, would have very simple business to perform. He would approach the barometer, examine it a moment, and return to give the public the results of his observation. But — such tricks of Fate do occur — perhaps the action takes place in a garden, and barometers do not grow on rosebushes. Then, rather than leave your character to wrestle with the difficulties of the first phrase, it would be correct to drag a barometer on to the stage, either under a far-fetched pretext or none at all. The audience will forgive this license more readily than they will a wait, or an obscurity, which are more dangerous faults.

Properties are of capital importance, and an author should make use of all his ingenuity to have them within reach in a plausible manner.

COSTUMES

The costumes should be as typical as possible, so as clearly to define at the first entrance, the station in life of the characters who wear them.

It is expedient for authors to choose their heroes from some job or profession which will easily be recognized from their distinctive garments. With the characters of the old Italian comedy there was no fear that Leander would be mistaken for Harlequin. In the time of Molière a marquis, a notary, an apothecary, a cloth merchant, etc., wore special costumes, which obviated all danger of confusion. But it is not so in this era; these different characters may all patronize the same tailor, and resemble each other like brothers.

Since there is the greatest necessity to initiate the audience instantly into the characteristics of a person as he enters, the artist should take the greatest pains in assembling his costume, adding to it all the marks, all the details, all the little trifles which can embody and explain the part he portrays.

The Use of Cosmetics

The use of cosmetics, that is to say, the actor's art of making-up, is of the greatest importance. On the stage, if an actor in a drama comes on in a costume and with a facial make-up not entirely appropriate to the rôle he represents — and this is too often witnessed — , the play will remain intelligible and will follow its course. But in a pantomime much more serious consequences might result from this.

An example will make this clear: — At a certain point a physician comes on the stage. In a play some actor can exclaim, " Ah, here's the dear doctor," or, " Come quickly, doctor, you are expected." That is sufficient; even should the actor in the rôle of physician more resemble a pianist the audience accepts him as one, even if it murmurs, " That's a queer make-up for a doctor."

But if the same thing happens in a pantomime, and at the entrance of the doctor the audience takes him for a pianist, a most unfortunate confusion will result, and perhaps, by a little ill-luck, a succession of atrocious misunderstandings, taking this for that, may follow, which will ruin the best of pantomimes.

The Bill of the Play

As nothing should be neglected which serves to enlighten the audience, authors are advised when writing up programs to return definitely to the style of Molière. As a typical example here is the list of characters in *George Dandin:*

George Dandin, wealthy farmer, husband of Angelique.

Angelique, wife of George Dandin, and daughter of M. de Sottenville.

M. de Sottenville, country gentleman, father of Angelique.

Mme. de Sottenville.

Clitandre, lover of Angelique.

Claudine, attendant of Angelique.

Lubin, peasant, Clitandre's servant.

Colin, valet of George Dandin.

The scene is in front of George Dandin's house in the country.

It would indeed be wrong to forego this method of enlightening the spectators, before the rise of the curtain, of the location of the act, the station in life of the characters, the relations between them; in fact, a good share of the exposition which costs the most trouble.

This method of writing the bill of the play, which has seemed a little too explicit for the modern theater, is still desirable for pantomimes. An audience will read a playbill and study a program; its coöperation extends thus far, but more must not be demanded of it.

This brings up another problem. Should an outline of plot be distributed to the spectators? that is, an explanation of the pantomime? Let the following syllogism give the answer. Either the pantomime is well constructed, that is to say, perfectly clear; or it is unintelligible, without a previous explanation.

In the first case, — the summary is not needed.

In the second case, — the pantomime should not be allowed on the boards.

So, no printed plot. Is it not a confession of weakness? Does it not warn the spectators that the author is incapable of putting over the show which the playbill announces? Is it not the same kind of folly that would lead a painter to write under his picture, " This represents a horse " ?

It is a true statement that a silent drama which is believed to need written explanation is not worth the trouble of putting on.

Imitative Sounds

In exceptional situations, and with great tact and caution, natural sounds such as cries, noises and imitations of noises, bursts of laughter, sobs, coughs, pst!, and exclamations, in short, all inarticulate sounds, may be used and high-grade effects produced.

Ah! Oh! Ough! express surprise, joy or pain.   The songs of birds, animal cries, the noise of instruments and tools, the rustling of silk, blasts of a whistle, etc., these, and the imitation of all sounds belong to the language of nature.   But they must be used with extreme delicacy.   Both author and actor must never forget that the silent drama is a kind of dream quietly unrolling before an audience, which must not be brutally awakened by a badly modulated noise.   Permissible sounds, including the music, should be only mystical noises, velvet sounds. This advice may seem very vague, but it will be thoroughly understood by those who have genuine theater-sense.

Another serious question pops up in this connection: May a pantomime make use of one speaking rôle? or of one line? or of one word?   No! a thousand times, No!   Not a rôle, not a line, not a word, not even if this single word should be needed to produce a profound sensation.   A single word would shatter brusquely the fragile charm built up with so much care.   Suspense, illusion, the dreamy feeling, would all fall in pieces and crumble before this clap of thunder.   The audience would not consent further to silence, dumbness would not be permitted, since this word has been spoken, why not all the rest?

A drama may permit one dumb character, as it does a deaf or blind one, as a type of infirmity, but, in a pantomime, a character who suddenly bursts into articulate language among characters who do not speak cannot be classed as infirm, even though he is the exception; it is an obnoxious absurdity.

While on this subject it may be added that to simulate speech is as absurd as to speak.   Some actors have been seen who actually try to play the silent drama, and who have formed the wretched habit of moving their lips and articulating without sounds the words they are portraying.   By what course of reasoning have they arrived at such an illogical conclusion?   Is it because they have heard that people who have lost their hearing learn to understand spoken words by the movement of the lips, so that they literally see speech and hear with their eyes?

But what connection can there be between this fact and pantomime? The audience is not deaf. Why simulate speech since you do not speak, since you must not speak, since, on the contrary, the talent of the actor seeks to make the existence of words temporarily forgotten? The use of such a silly method only produces the disagreeable impression that the actor wishes to speak but has lost his voice. Remember that a mime is not dumb, but a being apart, a mysterious creature having nothing to do with speech.

Another very important point is that while an actor yields himself to this silent loquacity, he denies himself the use of his lips and jaws whose movements concur powerfully in all facial expressions.

From the foregoing, it is easy to comprehend that it offends good taste equally to pretend to whisper in another's ear, or to listen in order to overhear a conversation. So these actions are absolutely forbidden:

To speak.

To simulate speech.

To simulate speaking in a low voice.

To simulate listening to a conversation.

CHAPTER VIII

STAGING THE PANTOMIME

Should an excellent pantomime be given over to a poor stage manager, a deplorable performance will result, but give a poor pantomime to a good director and he will make something interesting out of it.

Usually the author dictates the stage-setting and sometimes kills his own piece.

Every writer of a pantomime should be capable of being a professor of the art of mimicry, for his first difficulty will be the lack of mimes. His interpreters will be actors of more or less talent whose least fault will be that they believe a silent drama is not at all difficult to play. If the stage manager knows his business he will soon convince them of their error.

If a stage manager, trusting to his past experience and present inspiration, commences rehearsals without having prepared himself for his job by a very thorough study of the manuscript, he will not make good. He will inevitably make mistakes which will compel him to try experiments and change the stage business. This will delay the progress of the piece and permit the artists to make criticisms and even to interfere with the orders, which is fatal from every point of view. The stage manager can only acquire the full knowledge of what is best in the play, of all that needs to be done, of all that he must teach the actors, of all the perils to be avoided, of all the effects to be brought out, by studying thoroughly and in detail before the rehearsals, the play he must put on the boards.

He must know beforehand the dimensions of his stage, the exact location of each piece of furniture, and of every bit of property, and he must arrange them in such a manner that when the moment comes to make use of them, they will be found in the exact spot most convenient for the actors.

Besides, he must have determined from the point of view of physical exigency and of scenic effect, all the entrances, all the exits, all the crosses, and especially all the groupings, as well as the order in which these movements should be carried out, and he must never lose sight of the double obligation of facilitating the task of the interpreters and producing the strongest impression on the audience.

In short, the stage manager must know the piece from start to finish, especially wherein the principal movements are involved, as perfectly as if he had seen it performed a number of times.

It is a difficult, delicate and painstaking task and requires profound knowledge of the theater and its craft, but the resulting advantages cannot be measured.

The first effect will be to secure the confidence of the actors who will submit themselves blindly to the directions of a stage manager who knows what he wants and where he is going.

Right here it is well to draw the attention of authors and directors to a well recognized fact. Of all professions that of a dramatic artist is undoubtedly the one which rouses most actively the instinct of self-love, of desire for approbation. Is it because the actor or actress depends on physical attributes as well as intelligence to hold the interest of the audience? Possibly this is true. But whether it be through love of his or her art, through vanity, or through interest, it is a fact that every artist feels a thrill each time he is cast in a new rôle.

Is the play a good one? Will it be a success? Is this rôle the kind I will make a hit in? Is it all velvet? Such questions stir the actor's mind.

And, in fact, the prosperity of *his* theatrical life is at stake, it concerns his personal career, for a good rôle will bring him into prominence. Therefore it follows that on the day of the first rehearsal all the cast, the old as well as the young, arrive in a state of excitement that may be called the Fever of Art.

No zeal can compare with theirs. Anything may be demanded of them, they will attempt the impossible. Good actors, as well as poor ones, will surpass themselves. They are all impressionable.

If on his side the director arrives, armed on all points, if his directions are clear and definite, his commands logical, and his explanations irrefutable, if he is competent to point out to his interpreters business they had not foreseen, he will not be a stage manager who is obeyed grudgingly and mechanically, but he will be listened to and venerated as a master of the theater.

Instead of decreasing with subsequent rehearsals, this fever of emulation can only grow. Each one, in the part assigned to him, will bring an ardent zeal to the rounding out of the work, and with a surprising speed the piece will be learned, put on the stage and ready to be presented to the audience. Played under such conditions it will have the best chance of success.

If, on the contrary, the stage manager has not sufficiently prepared himself and is uncertain and perplexed, continual changes will result, and arguments will arise which will slow up the work considerably and depress the cast; and, finally, a performance which lacks this breath of enthusiasm and warm confidence will never get hold of the audience.

All that has been said up to now applies equally to spoken plays and pantomimes, but when questions of detail are broached, in addition to all the preceding, the stage manager of a silent drama must possess complete knowledge of the art of registering thoughts and feelings. It is not enough for him to tell an actor, " Your gesture is not clear, it means nothing," but he must be competent to teach him a better one.

First and foremost, the stage manager should require every actor, from his first entrance, to study the bearing, the walk and the habitual facial expression suitable to characterize the part he takes; as they say in France — to put himself under the skin of this character; as they say in America — Never drop out of character.

This first point is of prime importance and it is astonishing that it is not the object of special study in theaters where plays are produced.

A marquis and a butcher-boy, for instance, should differ even more by gait, posture, manners, the carriage of the head, the positions of arms and legs, and by the customary expression of face, than by the costume. This must be obtained before everything, and will immediately prove a big step in advance.

In the next place, without bothering about shades of expression, the director must work out the major action, that is, the entrances, exits, crosses, groups, the place the actors should stand during certain dialogues, the curves they should describe on the stage during such action, determine exactly when each shall sit or stand or assume some other posture. Only when this business has been established with almost geometrical precision, should the director take up the matter of expression.

If he is well versed in the principles of the art of registering emotion, contained in the first part of this book, he will find it easy to show the actors the movements indispensable to an accurate interpretation of their rôles. When this point is attained, a perfectly clear translation from the literary work into the language of pantomime, but with a mathematical want of decoration, has been created. Then and then only, may the director animate this skeleton of a play, inject into it life and intelligence by allowing the actors, who up to now have been automatons only, to demonstrate feeling, warmth and passion.

Another influence that will galvanize the pantomime is that the moment has arrived to join the music to the acting, to confine a certain series of gestures to a certain number of bars, and write a certain melody for a certain bit of business. This will bring about a complete transformation, and the performance will throb and grow eloquent. The last step will be to perfect the details and exact that the expressions and movements comprising them, have the required qualities.

For a *pantomimic expression* to be right it must be:

1st — Immediately and absolutely clear.

2nd — It must be impossible to impute to it a different meaning.

3rd — It must seem so simple and natural that no one gets the idea that speech would have been preferable.

Therefore, expressions which require too many explanatory gestures must be rejected or modified because they cause length. Also expressions whose meaning is equivocal, or which could signify several things, must be rejected or modified because they cause confusion.

Length and confusion are two dangers to be shunned.

A *pantomimic movement* should be executed with great precision.

Vague and incomplete movements are the same as to stammer and sputter spoken lines. They should be graceful. This quality will be acquired by the use of complementary movements whose object is to harmonize the whole body with the principal movement.

They must give the impression of the necessary accent or tone to accord with the nature of the sentiment expressed. Thus, the gesture meaning " Go! " may be made with sweetness, with kindness, with firmness, with hauteur, with scorn, etc. Between the first and the last emotion there is room for a crowd of shadings very desirable to see. They should have a certain time-limit; that is, a motionless pose sufficient to allow the spectator to see the actual gesticulation definitely and to distinguish it from the following. Gestures made too precipitately are lost.

The way to *end a phrase* when an actor has just completed a line in dumb show, or has been interrupted, is not to resume abruptly a neutral or waiting position; it is much better to hold the complete attitude he took when making the last gesture, and to let this attitude fade little by little until it disappears or is merged imperceptibly into the next meaningful pose. This method makes the actor's playing seem very natural and is strongly recommended.

Expression must have *unity*. Do not allow an actor, under

any circumstances, to express two things at one time. For instance, to the question, " You no longer need me? " to respond at the same time, " No " with the head and " Go! " with the arms.

Never suffer two or more actors to make gestures at the same time, even if they are in different groups and well separated from one another, for the simple reason that we hear a pantomime with our eyes. The eyes can perceive adequately only one gesture at a time. While the spectator is looking at a gesture being made on the right, if another is made on the left, it is true that it will be seen, he knows some one on the left has made a sign, but he will not have seen enough of it to understand its meaning. So the gesture on the left was of no use, since it could not be understood. Unfortunately, it is worse than useless, it is harmful. Because that portion of attention it exacted was subtracted from the total attention which it would have been desirable to concentrate on the gesture made on the right.

Suppose this fault happened frequently, as it inevitably will unless some one controls it and assures a better order, then, attracted by movements executed in the same period of time, the eye will rove wildly from person to person and from point to point, here and there, seeing first one and then another, preferably the most violent, and the mind will receive only confused ideas, absolutely unintelligible.

Therefore, only one actor should make expressive gesticulations at one time. It is impossible to imagine any situation which would permit an exception to this rule.

It is true that several actors, addressing the same person, may gesticulate at one time, to beg, injure or threaten him, but were there a hundred or a thousand of them they always represent one crowd, one group, one unity, in short, one speaker. And provided that this crowd and the person it is addressing do not gesticulate at the same time, but each in his turn, the dialogue will be as clear as if but two persons were on the stage.

GROUPING OF EXTRAS ON THE STAGE

As a general experience, stage managers do not give the requisite care and knowledge to the positions of extras and dancers on the stage, and to the movements required of them.

It would be delightful if each director were a painter of merit, for he must continually compose real stage pictures. And he need not disdain to consult the scene painters, who are nowadays men of great ability and talent, and whose advice would be very valuable, were it only as regards the proper perspective. Then, at least, one would no longer be distressed by such faults as the following example illustrates:

The scenery represents a countryside. By an admirable effect of perspective, the view extends to a great distance. The stage is full of extra players. In similar cases it has often been noticed that the shorter people have been placed in the foreground and the tallest at the rear of the stage, against the back drop. Now, good taste and judgment compel absolutely the contrary arrangement.

Would that theatrical producers could be imbued with this idea, that it is their mission to build up a succession of interesting stage tableaux, and thus employ with great art the powerful resources in their hands.

On the other hand, their attention is earnestly called to scenes of general action, which may be classed as scenes of tumult or mob-scenes. These are precisely those calling for the most order, method and care in the details.

For such situations a director who will cry, as has happened many times, " Go, run, agitate yourselves, throw yourselves about! " is a man who does not know his trade. Whether the boards are to set forth a lively fête, a riot, or a scene of the height of disorder, not a single action must be permitted that was not pointed out, and set in its place in the sequence of all the other movements. This is easy to conceive, because the director is under the necessity of giving the audience a sensation accurately planned, so all movements executed must concur in giving this sensation. The total incoherence necessarily resulting from movements done from an individual's initiative, whatever amount of zeal and intelligence he may possess, produces nothing, not even the impression of disorder: the outcome will be inartistic, negative as regards effect, and thoroughly unpleasant to witness.

As a general rule, be very cautious about action, because of the power of action.

In some situations a mere wink of the eye may produce a stronger effect than a hundred men ranting to the utmost.

For the final word, then, let the spectacle of a pantomime be a series of moving pictures which each gesture changes every moment, but not incessantly, for they must contain short periods of immobility when they *hold the pose.*

In addition to this ordinary holding of the pose, the stage manager will come across certain points in any pantomime which may be called *major moments,* either due to the intensity of the action of the play, or to the importance resulting from the total attitudes of all the characters. In order to distinguish these moments and get their full value across, he need only prolong the usual pause of gesture into a kind of *high point,* that is, to increase by several seconds the usual wait following each one's last gesture which will produce for a brief period, a genuine living picture. (Tableau vivant.)

Well-spaced, well-chosen, and carried out with tact, these effects of the pause cannot fail to get over the footlights.

CHAPTER IX

THE ACCOMPANIMENT OF MUSIC

When present at a performance of a drama played in a foreign tongue, the spectator first experiences a sense of disturbance from hearing words spoken whose meaning is unknown. But, as the mind gives up, little by little, the habitual effort to attach precise meaning to the spoken word, he soon perceives only the picture, the movements, and the action, and the oratory of the players becomes a sort of song composed of modulations, sometimes soft and tender as prayers, and again bitter and fierce as the cries of anger. Finally the drama becomes a kind of play without words whose music is the voice of the actors.

It is the author's belief that the real mission of music in a pantomime is to take the place of the voice of the characters and to render this same inarticulate eloquence, these emotional modulations which are the natural expressions of human feeling.

The tragedian Rossi bequeathed an absolutely unforgettable impression. At the moment of killing Desdemona he stood at the front of the stage and, without a motion, but with his face frightfully distorted, he sent forth a prolonged moan, weak at first, but which grew stronger and stronger until it burst into a kind of fearful roar: and when, all of a sudden, he disappeared behind the curtain which concealed the bed where Desdemona lay, everyone saw in all its horror the deed he did there. No line, no powerful and perfect literary expression, could produce such emotion as this cry without a word, a syllable. This cry was like the music which portrays an emotion.

Should a pantomime be accompanied by an orchestra or simply by a piano?

If, after what has just been said, music is acknowledged to

be the voice of the mime, it must be admitted the piano does not fulfil the desired object.

When nothing else can be obtained, it will have to satisfy, it is always better than a drum; but a musician who can secure an orchestra, even a simple quartette, would do wrong to prefer a piano under the trifling pretext that with this instrument alone it is easier to follow the actor's play.

Should the " *Leit-Motif* " be employed?

Certainly, it is emphatically called for. Should not a character have a personality distinguishing him from the others in the cast?

It may be presumptuous to advise, but musical composers are recommended to associate more definitely with each of the cast an instrument typical of the character: as the flute for the maiden, the cello for the lover, the bassoon for the old father, the clarinet for the funny man — etc.

At what time should the music of a pantomime be composed?

The custom is to proceed with a pantomime as with a ballet. When the author has finished his script he confides it to a musician who writes the music for it according to his fancy, following his own notions of the interpretation of a work in dumb show. The outcome of this is, that before even the first rehearsal, the producer is confronted by a play within strict limitations which must be interpreted just as it is. This could only prove the correct method if the author had not committed the least error, and if the musical composers were gifted with a miraculous intuition as to all the acting that would be found necessary — of all the gestures that ought to be made, their number, their degree, and their duration, so that he should not write one bar too many, nor one bar too few. In other words, the author and the composer would have to possess, both of them equally, not only a complete experience of pantomime, but an infallible knowledge of the art.

Can it be hoped that such is always the case?

Far from it. Due to this very impractical method of collaboration, what usually happens is this: From the very first rehearsal the artist finds his work constricted by the music as by a too narrow suit of armor. He has no liberty to seek truthful expressions or the correct kind and length of gesture; he is solely under the obligation to follow the music, whatever it is. He is continually forced to present within four bars a scene which requires thirty, or to fill in thirty bars, no matter how, with work for which four would have given sufficient time. From this two serious faults inevitably result: first, phrases insufficiently outlined which cause misunderstanding; and second, others irksomely repeated which cause the show to drag.

Here is what actually happened to a ballet-pantomime in one of the principal theaters of Paris. For the entrance of the recruiting sergeant, an important rôle, the musician had composed a march of 32 measures, a quickstep of charm. The sergeant enters with many airs. At the end of the 4th measure he has arrived at the prompter's box, and twenty-eight bars are still to be played. The director reproaches him: " You came down stage too fast. Once more."

The sergeant moderates his gait; he even halts a moment on the way, and still finds himself in front of the prompter's box at the eighth bar of music. The musician cries: " There are still twenty-four bars to be played." Then the director advises the actor to bow to right and left where the promenaders and small merchants come and go on the stage; also the dancers are ordered to step in front of the sergeant and surround him. The sergeant begins all over and this time does not arrive at the footlights until the 16th bar. Still there are sixteen measures too many. The musician storms, the director loudly expresses his astonishment at the actor's awkwardness. The sergeant has lost his air of bravado, he swallows a just imprecation.

Nevertheless, he starts his entrance again, and on the signals of the ballet-mistress and director, he bows to right and left; he chucks the chin of a flower-girl, then of another; he waves some vague gestures. Seeing that in spite of all this he is already drawing near the footlights, he steps up quickly towards the group on the left which he salutes, then he salutes the group on the right likewise; then he taps a cheek here and there. His face expresses just one thing, " Is this music ever going to end? " Alas, no, there is more of it. So he bows very courteously, and bows and bows. Never was there so polite a soldier.

At last the thirty-two bars are ended, the action is about to take place.

The handsome recruiting officer must get a young villager drunk and persuade him to sign up for the Army. Now, unfortunately, the opposite fault prevails and there is not enough music. The unlucky sergeant must hurry, quicken his gestures, and has not expressed a quarter of what he should before the music for the following scene commences.

The director pushes the action, cuts and shortens it to the point where the scene loses its significance. And some day this director will say, " It's odd that the public doesn't like pantomimes."

What is indeed odd is to dare produce a spectacle when one understands nothing about it. As a matter of fact, it is not the composer of the music who is to blame, but the author whose manuscript is so unfinished that no one can draw definite information from it.

It is worth while to repeat, that the prime necessity is that the play should be completely written out, the dialogues of scenes as for a drama, and that it must contain all the ideas which need to be acted out in dumb show.

Only then should the author approach the musical composer, and dramatize his play from beginning to end before him. Then the two should decide, bit by bit, the sentiment and the duration of the music for each movement, each action, each line.

The composer should make a plot of the whole score. That is, should outline as a whole the style, the motifs, the movements and desirable effects. He should note exactly what number of bars of music are necessary for a certain movement, a certain action, a certain line.

So the writer must be capable of acting out his script, at least from the viewpoint of time required for each expression, or else he should bring with him an experienced pantomimist. Undoubtedly this is a troublesome and difficult task, but it is the only method to attain a satisfactory result.

While the composer is writing the score, the author can begin to put on the play and teach his interpreters what is expected of them.

This work carried out in silence is excellent, because it allows the writer to polish up belated details and to interrupt as many times as is necessary with more ease than if the musician were present.

When at last the day of the first rehearsal with music arrives, in spite of all the precautions taken, the director must expect some surprises and slight misfits.

This first trial of associating the acting, free up to this time, with the music, will produce a certain nervousness in both actors and author. But thanks to this plan, if used, the difficulties will only be slight. Gradually, by mutual concessions, they will grow into unity; the gesture will be molded by the musical phrase, and the musical phrase will become the voice of the gesture and everyone will be thrilled with rare joy in seeing the play suddenly come to life, and become warm, eloquent and vital.

The pantomime should not submit to the rule of the music, but the music should subordinate itself to the demands of the pantomime.

The next point is to determine what variety of music is appropriate to a silent drama.

For a long time pantomimists have had to be content with any kind of a dance tune played over and over until the fall of the curtain, which was actually a hindrance rather than a help.

Some authors of today, falling into the opposite extreme, declare that every movement, excepting none, should be minutely detailed by the accompaniment.

Evidently these latter are nearer the truth, but exaggeration in this direction may also become a fault.

Pantomimes may be divided into three varieties of scenes for the consideration of the composer.

1st — *Scenes of Preparatory Action,* which do not need to be musically indicated in detail. For instance:

" The servant lays the table ": It would be perfectly childish to have him place each knife and fork in time to a set note. Or —

" The newly-wed receives the guests." Would it not be ridiculous to make the guests sit down in a rhythmical manner?

A motif which interprets the general sentiment of the scene is quite sufficient up to the moment when the plot takes a more active turn.

2nd — *Scenes of Action,* which comprise all movements having important meanings; all decisive gestures; all really dramatic scenes. It is readily understood that these have everything to gain by being aligned in detail with special motifs; by longer or shorter melodies; or by simple chords.

3rd — *Scenes of Dialogue.* The dialogue of a pantomime should be treated just like the recitative of an opera. The composer can let himself go with all possible spirit and inspiration, provided he keeps within the limits of the acted line, whose length often differs noticeably from the spoken line.

There is an effective device which might be called the *acted-out song.* It is a succession of ideas cut out of several scenes by a unique refrain. The author must lead up to this effect and the musician grasp it.

Finally the use of a very powerful aid, *Silence.*

Absolute silence abruptly following the sound of the orchestra attracts attention more than the report of a gun. Therefore this effect must be reserved for scenes of the greatest interest. For instance, a character has to commit a murder; the victim, unaware of the danger threatening him, is three steps from the assassin. While this latter takes these three steps, while he lifts his dagger, and until the moment he strikes, silence is infinitely more eloquent than any orchestral effect possible.

Silence is Holding the Breath; and this definition gives the maximum length of a silence. A last thought on the subject of the accompaniment of music is: it is not sufficient for the composer to have talent to make a good score for a pantomime, he must also have enough self-abnegation to deny himself rigorously all effects of his art, even the most excellent, which might draw special approbation to the music, and, in consequence, would distract the spectator's state of mind which is always supposed to be under the spell of a dream.

This does not mean the musician should avoid making use of his full talent, but rather that the proofs of his highest ability be so perfectly adapted to the dramatic action that the benefit extends to the whole work.

CHAPTER X

THE BALLET

Little will be said on this subject. Ballets consist of acted
scenes and dancing scenes. The acted scenes of a ballet should
be played exactly like the scenes of a pantomime and all that
has been said in this book applies to them.

As the dancing scenes are governed specifically by the principles of their own art, their discussion does not belong here.

Nevertheless, when considering that French ballets are becoming inferior to those of other nations, that the public has
lost interest, and frankly declares itself bored, that it must be
inferred that this is because people really are bored; that this
is due less to the inadequacy of the dancers as such than to the
dull, commonplaceness and confusion of the action, it may be
well to express some earnest wishes.

If only directors would cease thinking that it is sufficient to
exhibit pretty girls in rather suggestive costumes which serve
to display their natural charms, and require these ladies to
know how to act and dance.

If they would only recognize their mistake in believing that
the libretto of a ballet is of no importance; that it can be
patched up in a few lines requiring no special knowledge, and
thus may be requested from any friend they wish to please,
or to the first comer it is to their interest to gratify.

If they would finally give up trying, without understanding anything about it, to put the show on by themselves, instead
of turning it over to men of professional experience.

The union of dancing, acting and music can produce the most
graceful and enchanting spectacles. It is a very delicate art
which demands special talents and infinite taste. In the hands

of an ignoramus the results are flat, tedious, and even repellent, for, in spite of oneself, one is indignant to see valuable resources squandered through stupidity. Usually the scenery is marvelous, the costumes exquisite, and the musical score charming, only the libretto and the direction of the work are worthless.

Without going into details, these observations are addressed to authors of ballets:

A ballet should be a play.

Of course its subject should be rather simple and pleasing but still it demands the same qualities of clearness and interest as any other kind of play. Its means of expression are pantomime and dancing. Hence this acting and dancing must express something, must mean something.

The corps de ballet must have a reason for being in motion. The dance should harmonize with the action.

It is well understood that a dancing scene can be only a scene capable of expression by dancing; but nevertheless, this scene must be pertinent to the entire plan. So dancing must be regarded as a means of expression, as having the same title as pantomime to be called a language, and not merely a brilliant exercise, without significance, and similar to any acrobatic interlude. Therefore, authors and stage managers, before assuming to compose and regulate ballets, should first learn what dancing and pantomime really consist of, and know the art of using them as means of expression. Then only can the public hope to witness interesting ballets.

A CATALOG OF SELECTED

DOVER BOOKS

IN ALL FIELDS OF INTEREST

A CATALOG OF SELECTED DOVER
BOOKS IN ALL FIELDS OF INTEREST

CONCERNING THE SPIRITUAL IN ART, Wassily Kandinsky. Pioneering work by father of abstract art. Thoughts on color theory, nature of art. Analysis of earlier masters. 12 illustrations. 80pp. of text. 5⅜ x 8½. 23411-8

ANIMALS: 1,419 Copyright-Free Illustrations of Mammals, Birds, Fish, Insects, etc., Jim Harter (ed.). Clear wood engravings present, in extremely lifelike poses, over 1,000 species of animals. One of the most extensive pictorial sourcebooks of its kind. Captions. Index. 284pp. 9 x 12. 23766-4

CELTIC ART: The Methods of Construction, George Bain. Simple geometric techniques for making Celtic interlacements, spirals, Kells-type initials, animals, humans, etc. Over 500 illustrations. 160pp. 9 x 12. (Available in U.S. only.) 22923-8

AN ATLAS OF ANATOMY FOR ARTISTS, Fritz Schider. Most thorough reference work on art anatomy in the world. Hundreds of illustrations, including selections from works by Vesalius, Leonardo, Goya, Ingres, Michelangelo, others. 593 illustrations. 192pp. 7⅛ x 10¼. 20241-0

CELTIC HAND STROKE-BY-STROKE (Irish Half-Uncial from "The Book of Kells"): An Arthur Baker Calligraphy Manual, Arthur Baker. Complete guide to creating each letter of the alphabet in distinctive Celtic manner. Covers hand position, strokes, pens, inks, paper, more. Illustrated. 48pp. 8¼ x 11. 24336-2

EASY ORIGAMI, John Montroll. Charming collection of 32 projects (hat, cup, pelican, piano, swan, many more) specially designed for the novice origami hobbyist. Clearly illustrated easy-to-follow instructions insure that even beginning papercrafters will achieve successful results. 48pp. 8¼ x 11. 27298-2

THE COMPLETE BOOK OF BIRDHOUSE CONSTRUCTION FOR WOODWORKERS, Scott D. Campbell. Detailed instructions, illustrations, tables. Also data on bird habitat and instinct patterns. Bibliography. 3 tables. 63 illustrations in 15 figures. 48pp. 5¼ x 8½. 24407-5

BLOOMINGDALE'S ILLUSTRATED 1886 CATALOG: Fashions, Dry Goods and Housewares, Bloomingdale Brothers. Famed merchants' extremely rare catalog depicting about 1,700 products: clothing, housewares, firearms, dry goods, jewelry, more. Invaluable for dating, identifying vintage items. Also, copyright-free graphics for artists, designers. Co-published with Henry Ford Museum & Greenfield Village. 160pp. 8¼ x 11. 25780-0

HISTORIC COSTUME IN PICTURES, Braun & Schneider. Over 1,450 costumed figures in clearly detailed engravings–from dawn of civilization to end of 19th century. Captions. Many folk costumes. 256pp. 8⅜ x 11¾. 23150-X

STICKLEY CRAFTSMAN FURNITURE CATALOGS, Gustav Stickley and L. & J. G. Stickley. Beautiful, functional furniture in two authentic catalogs from 1910. 594 illustrations, including 277 photos, show settles, rockers, armchairs, reclining chairs, bookcases, desks, tables. 183pp. 6½ x 9¼. 23838-5

AMERICAN LOCOMOTIVES IN HISTORIC PHOTOGRAPHS: 1858 to 1949, Ron Ziel (ed.). A rare collection of 126 meticulously detailed official photographs, called "builder portraits," of American locomotives that majestically chronicle the rise of steam locomotive power in America. Introduction. Detailed captions. xi+ 129pp. 9 x 12. 27393-8

AMERICA'S LIGHTHOUSES: An Illustrated History, Francis Ross Holland, Jr. Delightfully written, profusely illustrated fact-filled survey of over 200 American lighthouses since 1716. History, anecdotes, technological advances, more. 240pp. 8 x 10¾. 25576-X

TOWARDS A NEW ARCHITECTURE, Le Corbusier. Pioneering manifesto by founder of "International School." Technical and aesthetic theories, views of industry, economics, relation of form to function, "mass-production split" and much more. Profusely illustrated. 320pp. 6⅛ x 9¼. (Available in U.S. only.) 25023-7

HOW THE OTHER HALF LIVES, Jacob Riis. Famous journalistic record, exposing poverty and degradation of New York slums around 1900, by major social reformer. 100 striking and influential photographs. 233pp. 10 x 7⅞. 22012-5

FRUIT KEY AND TWIG KEY TO TREES AND SHRUBS, William M. Harlow. One of the handiest and most widely used identification aids. Fruit key covers 120 deciduous and evergreen species; twig key 160 deciduous species. Easily used. Over 300 photographs. 126pp. 5⅜ x 8½. 20511-8

COMMON BIRD SONGS, Dr. Donald J. Borror. Songs of 60 most common U.S. birds: robins, sparrows, cardinals, bluejays, finches, more–arranged in order of increasing complexity. Up to 9 variations of songs of each species.

Cassette and manual 99911-4

ORCHIDS AS HOUSE PLANTS, Rebecca Tyson Northen. Grow cattleyas and many other kinds of orchids–in a window, in a case, or under artificial light. 63 illustrations. 148pp. 5⅜ x 8½. 23261-1

MONSTER MAZES, Dave Phillips. Masterful mazes at four levels of difficulty. Avoid deadly perils and evil creatures to find magical treasures. Solutions for all 32 exciting illustrated puzzles. 48pp. 8¼ x 11. 26005-4

MOZART'S DON GIOVANNI (DOVER OPERA LIBRETTO SERIES), Wolfgang Amadeus Mozart. Introduced and translated by Ellen H. Bleiler. Standard Italian libretto, with complete English translation. Convenient and thoroughly portable–an ideal companion for reading along with a recording or the performance itself. Introduction. List of characters. Plot summary. 121pp. 5¼ x 8½. 24944-1

TECHNICAL MANUAL AND DICTIONARY OF CLASSICAL BALLET, Gail Grant. Defines, explains, comments on steps, movements, poses and concepts. 15-page pictorial section. Basic book for student, viewer. 127pp. 5⅜ x 8½. 21843-0

THE CLARINET AND CLARINET PLAYING, David Pino. Lively, comprehensive work features suggestions about technique, musicianship, and musical interpretation, as well as guidelines for teaching, making your own reeds, and preparing for public performance. Includes an intriguing look at clarinet history. "A godsend," *The Clarinet,* Journal of the International Clarinet Society. Appendixes. 7 illus. 320pp. 5⅜ x 8½. 40270-3

HOLLYWOOD GLAMOR PORTRAITS, John Kobal (ed.). 145 photos from 1926-49. Harlow, Gable, Bogart, Bacall; 94 stars in all. Full background on photographers, technical aspects. 160pp. 8⅜ x 11¼. 23352-9

THE ANNOTATED CASEY AT THE BAT: A Collection of Ballads about the Mighty Casey/Third, Revised Edition, Martin Gardner (ed.). Amusing sequels and parodies of one of America's best-loved poems: Casey's Revenge, Why Casey Whiffed, Casey's Sister at the Bat, others. 256pp. 5⅜ x 8½. 28598-7

THE RAVEN AND OTHER FAVORITE POEMS, Edgar Allan Poe. Over 40 of the author's most memorable poems: "The Bells," "Ulalume," "Israfel," "To Helen," "The Conqueror Worm," "Eldorado," "Annabel Lee," many more. Alphabetic lists of titles and first lines. 64pp. 5$\frac{3}{16}$ x 8¼. 26685-0

PERSONAL MEMOIRS OF U. S. GRANT, Ulysses Simpson Grant. Intelligent, deeply moving firsthand account of Civil War campaigns, considered by many the finest military memoirs ever written. Includes letters, historic photographs, maps and more. 528pp. 6⅛ x 9¼. 28587-1

ANCIENT EGYPTIAN MATERIALS AND INDUSTRIES, A. Lucas and J. Harris. Fascinating, comprehensive, thoroughly documented text describes this ancient civilization's vast resources and the processes that incorporated them in daily life, including the use of animal products, building materials, cosmetics, perfumes and incense, fibers, glazed ware, glass and its manufacture, materials used in the mummification process, and much more. 544pp. 6⅛ x 9¼. (Available in U.S. only.) 40446-3

RUSSIAN STORIES/RUSSKIE RASSKAZY: A Dual-Language Book, edited by Gleb Struve. Twelve tales by such masters as Chekhov, Tolstoy, Dostoevsky, Pushkin, others. Excellent word-for-word English translations on facing pages, plus teaching and study aids, Russian/English vocabulary, biographical/critical introductions, more. 416pp. 5⅜ x 8½. 26244-8

PHILADELPHIA THEN AND NOW: 60 Sites Photographed in the Past and Present, Kenneth Finkel and Susan Oyama. Rare photographs of City Hall, Logan Square, Independence Hall, Betsy Ross House, other landmarks juxtaposed with contemporary views. Captures changing face of historic city. Introduction. Captions. 128pp. 8¼ x 11. 25790-8

AIA ARCHITECTURAL GUIDE TO NASSAU AND SUFFOLK COUNTIES, LONG ISLAND, The American Institute of Architects, Long Island Chapter, and the Society for the Preservation of Long Island Antiquities. Comprehensive, well-researched and generously illustrated volume brings to life over three centuries of Long Island's great architectural heritage. More than 240 photographs with authoritative, extensively detailed captions. 176pp. 8¼ x 11. 26946-9

NORTH AMERICAN INDIAN LIFE: Customs and Traditions of 23 Tribes, Elsie Clews Parsons (ed.). 27 fictionalized essays by noted anthropologists examine religion, customs, government, additional facets of life among the Winnebago, Crow, Zuni, Eskimo, other tribes. 480pp. 6⅛ x 9¼. 27377-6

FRANK LLOYD WRIGHT'S DANA HOUSE, Donald Hoffmann. Pictorial essay of residential masterpiece with over 160 interior and exterior photos, plans, elevations, sketches and studies. 128pp. 9¼ x 10¾.   29120-0

THE MALE AND FEMALE FIGURE IN MOTION: 60 Classic Photographic Sequences, Eadweard Muybridge. 60 true-action photographs of men and women walking, running, climbing, bending, turning, etc., reproduced from rare 19th-century masterpiece. vi + 121pp. 9 x 12.   24745-7

1001 QUESTIONS ANSWERED ABOUT THE SEASHORE, N. J. Berrill and Jacquelyn Berrill. Queries answered about dolphins, sea snails, sponges, starfish, fishes, shore birds, many others. Covers appearance, breeding, growth, feeding, much more. 305pp. 5¼ x 8¼.   23366-9

ATTRACTING BIRDS TO YOUR YARD, William J. Weber. Easy-to-follow guide offers advice on how to attract the greatest diversity of birds: birdhouses, feeders, water and waterers, much more. 96pp. 5³⁄₁₆ x 8¼.   28927-3

MEDICINAL AND OTHER USES OF NORTH AMERICAN PLANTS: A Historical Survey with Special Reference to the Eastern Indian Tribes, Charlotte Erichsen-Brown. Chronological historical citations document 500 years of usage of plants, trees, shrubs native to eastern Canada, northeastern U.S. Also complete identifying information. 343 illustrations. 544pp. 6½ x 9¼.   25951-X

STORYBOOK MAZES, Dave Phillips. 23 stories and mazes on two-page spreads: Wizard of Oz, Treasure Island, Robin Hood, etc. Solutions. 64pp. 8¼ x 11. 23628-5

AMERICAN NEGRO SONGS: 230 Folk Songs and Spirituals, Religious and Secular, John W. Work. This authoritative study traces the African influences of songs sung and played by black Americans at work, in church, and as entertainment. The author discusses the lyric significance of such songs as "Swing Low, Sweet Chariot," "John Henry," and others and offers the words and music for 230 songs. Bibliography. Index of Song Titles. 272pp. 6½ x 9¼.   40271-1

MOVIE-STAR PORTRAITS OF THE FORTIES, John Kobal (ed.). 163 glamor, studio photos of 106 stars of the 1940s: Rita Hayworth, Ava Gardner, Marlon Brando, Clark Gable, many more. 176pp. 8⅜ x 11¼.   23546-7

BENCHLEY LOST AND FOUND, Robert Benchley. Finest humor from early 30s, about pet peeves, child psychologists, post office and others. Mostly unavailable elsewhere. 73 illustrations by Peter Arno and others. 183pp. 5⅜ x 8½.   22410-4

YEKL and THE IMPORTED BRIDEGROOM AND OTHER STORIES OF YIDDISH NEW YORK, Abraham Cahan. Film Hester Street based on *Yekl* (1896). Novel, other stories among first about Jewish immigrants on N.Y.'s East Side. 240pp. 5⅜ x 8½.   22427-9

SELECTED POEMS, Walt Whitman. Generous sampling from *Leaves of Grass*. Twenty-four poems include "I Hear America Singing," "Song of the Open Road," "I Sing the Body Electric," "When Lilacs Last in the Dooryard Bloom'd," "O Captain! My Captain!"–all reprinted from an authoritative edition. Lists of titles and first lines. 128pp. 5³⁄₁₆ x 8¼.   26878-0

THE BEST TALES OF HOFFMANN, E. T. A. Hoffmann. 10 of Hoffmann's most important stories: "Nutcracker and the King of Mice," "The Golden Flowerpot," etc. 458pp. 5⅜ x 8½. 21793-0

FROM FETISH TO GOD IN ANCIENT EGYPT, E. A. Wallis Budge. Rich detailed survey of Egyptian conception of "God" and gods, magic, cult of animals, Osiris, more. Also, superb English translations of hymns and legends. 240 illustrations. 545pp. 5⅜ x 8½. 25803-3

FRENCH STORIES/CONTES FRANÇAIS: A Dual-Language Book, Wallace Fowlie. Ten stories by French masters, Voltaire to Camus: "Micromegas" by Voltaire; "The Atheist's Mass" by Balzac; "Minuet" by de Maupassant; "The Guest" by Camus, six more. Excellent English translations on facing pages. Also French-English vocabulary list, exercises, more. 352pp. 5⅜ x 8½. 26443-2

CHICAGO AT THE TURN OF THE CENTURY IN PHOTOGRAPHS: 122 Historic Views from the Collections of the Chicago Historical Society, Larry A. Viskochil. Rare large-format prints offer detailed views of City Hall, State Street, the Loop, Hull House, Union Station, many other landmarks, circa 1904-1913. Introduction. Captions. Maps. 144pp. 9⅜ x 12¼. 24656-6

OLD BROOKLYN IN EARLY PHOTOGRAPHS, 1865-1929, William Lee Younger. Luna Park, Gravesend race track, construction of Grand Army Plaza, moving of Hotel Brighton, etc. 157 previously unpublished photographs. 165pp. 8⅞ x 11¾. 23587-4

THE MYTHS OF THE NORTH AMERICAN INDIANS, Lewis Spence. Rich anthology of the myths and legends of the Algonquins, Iroquois, Pawnees and Sioux, prefaced by an extensive historical and ethnological commentary. 36 illustrations. 480pp. 5⅜ x 8½. 25967-6

AN ENCYCLOPEDIA OF BATTLES: Accounts of Over 1,560 Battles from 1479 B.C. to the Present, David Eggenberger. Essential details of every major battle in recorded history from the first battle of Megiddo in 1479 B.C. to Grenada in 1984. List of Battle Maps. New Appendix covering the years 1967-1984. Index. 99 illustrations. 544pp. 6½ x 9¼. 24913-1

SAILING ALONE AROUND THE WORLD, Captain Joshua Slocum. First man to sail around the world, alone, in small boat. One of great feats of seamanship told in delightful manner. 67 illustrations. 294pp. 5⅜ x 8½. 20326-3

ANARCHISM AND OTHER ESSAYS, Emma Goldman. Powerful, penetrating, prophetic essays on direct action, role of minorities, prison reform, puritan hypocrisy, violence, etc. 271pp. 5⅜ x 8½. 22484-8

MYTHS OF THE HINDUS AND BUDDHISTS, Ananda K. Coomaraswamy and Sister Nivedita. Great stories of the epics; deeds of Krishna, Shiva, taken from puranas, Vedas, folk tales; etc. 32 illustrations. 400pp. 5⅜ x 8½. 21759-0

THE TRAUMA OF BIRTH, Otto Rank. Rank's controversial thesis that anxiety neurosis is caused by profound psychological trauma which occurs at birth. 256pp. 5⅜ x 8½. 27974-X

A THEOLOGICO-POLITICAL TREATISE, Benedict Spinoza. Also contains unfinished Political Treatise. Great classic on religious liberty, theory of government on common consent. R. Elwes translation. Total of 421pp. 5⅜ x 8½. 20249-6

MY BONDAGE AND MY FREEDOM, Frederick Douglass. Born a slave, Douglass became outspoken force in antislavery movement. The best of Douglass' autobiographies. Graphic description of slave life. 464pp. 5⅜ x 8½. 22457-0

FOLLOWING THE EQUATOR: A Journey Around the World, Mark Twain. Fascinating humorous account of 1897 voyage to Hawaii, Australia, India, New Zealand, etc. Ironic, bemused reports on peoples, customs, climate, flora and fauna, politics, much more. 197 illustrations. 720pp. 5⅜ x 8½. 26113-1

THE PEOPLE CALLED SHAKERS, Edward D. Andrews. Definitive study of Shakers: origins, beliefs, practices, dances, social organization, furniture and crafts, etc. 33 illustrations. 351pp. 5⅜ x 8½. 21081-2

THE MYTHS OF GREECE AND ROME, H. A. Guerber. A classic of mythology, generously illustrated, long prized for its simple, graphic, accurate retelling of the principal myths of Greece and Rome, and for its commentary on their origins and significance. With 64 illustrations by Michelangelo, Raphael, Titian, Rubens, Canova, Bernini and others. 480pp. 5⅜ x 8½. 27584-1

PSYCHOLOGY OF MUSIC, Carl E. Seashore. Classic work discusses music as a medium from psychological viewpoint. Clear treatment of physical acoustics, auditory apparatus, sound perception, development of musical skills, nature of musical feeling, host of other topics. 88 figures. 408pp. 5⅜ x 8½. 21851-1

THE PHILOSOPHY OF HISTORY, Georg W. Hegel. Great classic of Western thought develops concept that history is not chance but rational process, the evolution of freedom. 457pp. 5⅜ x 8½. 20112-0

THE BOOK OF TEA, Kakuzo Okakura. Minor classic of the Orient: entertaining, charming explanation, interpretation of traditional Japanese culture in terms of tea ceremony. 94pp. 5⅜ x 8½. 20070-1

LIFE IN ANCIENT EGYPT, Adolf Erman. Fullest, most thorough, detailed older account with much not in more recent books, domestic life, religion, magic, medicine, commerce, much more. Many illustrations reproduce tomb paintings, carvings, hieroglyphs, etc. 597pp. 5⅜ x 8½. 22632-8

SUNDIALS, Their Theory and Construction, Albert Waugh. Far and away the best, most thorough coverage of ideas, mathematics concerned, types, construction, adjusting anywhere. Simple, nontechnical treatment allows even children to build several of these dials. Over 100 illustrations. 230pp. 5⅜ x 8½. 22947-5

THEORETICAL HYDRODYNAMICS, L. M. Milne-Thomson. Classic exposition of the mathematical theory of fluid motion, applicable to both hydrodynamics and aerodynamics. Over 600 exercises. 768pp. 6⅛ x 9¼. 68970-0

SONGS OF EXPERIENCE: Facsimile Reproduction with 26 Plates in Full Color, William Blake. 26 full-color plates from a rare 1826 edition. Includes "The Tyger," "London," "Holy Thursday," and other poems. Printed text of poems. 48pp. 5¼ x 7. 24636-1

OLD-TIME VIGNETTES IN FULL COLOR, Carol Belanger Grafton (ed.). Over 390 charming, often sentimental illustrations, selected from archives of Victorian graphics—pretty women posing, children playing, food, flowers, kittens and puppies, smiling cherubs, birds and butterflies, much more. All copyright-free. 48pp. 9¼ x 12¼. 27269-9

PERSPECTIVE FOR ARTISTS, Rex Vicat Cole. Depth, perspective of sky and sea, shadows, much more, not usually covered. 391 diagrams, 81 reproductions of drawings and paintings. 279pp. 5⅜ x 8½. 22487-2

DRAWING THE LIVING FIGURE, Joseph Sheppard. Innovative approach to artistic anatomy focuses on specifics of surface anatomy, rather than muscles and bones. Over 170 drawings of live models in front, back and side views, and in widely varying poses. Accompanying diagrams. 177 illustrations. Introduction. Index. 144pp. 8⅜ x11¼. 26723-7

GOTHIC AND OLD ENGLISH ALPHABETS: 100 Complete Fonts, Dan X. Solo. Add power, elegance to posters, signs, other graphics with 100 stunning copyright-free alphabets: Blackstone, Dolbey, Germania, 97 more–including many lower-case, numerals, punctuation marks. 104pp. 8⅛ x 11. 24695-7

HOW TO DO BEADWORK, Mary White. Fundamental book on craft from simple projects to five-bead chains and woven works. 106 illustrations. 142pp. 5⅜ x 8. 20697-1

THE BOOK OF WOOD CARVING, Charles Marshall Sayers. Finest book for beginners discusses fundamentals and offers 34 designs. "Absolutely first rate . . . well thought out and well executed."–E. J. Tangerman. 118pp. 7¾ x 10⅝. 23654-4

ILLUSTRATED CATALOG OF CIVIL WAR MILITARY GOODS: Union Army Weapons, Insignia, Uniform Accessories, and Other Equipment, Schuyler, Hartley, and Graham. Rare, profusely illustrated 1846 catalog includes Union Army uniform and dress regulations, arms and ammunition, coats, insignia, flags, swords, rifles, etc. 226 illustrations. 160pp. 9 x 12. 24939-5

WOMEN'S FASHIONS OF THE EARLY 1900s: An Unabridged Republication of "New York Fashions, 1909," National Cloak & Suit Co. Rare catalog of mail-order fashions documents women's and children's clothing styles shortly after the turn of the century. Captions offer full descriptions, prices. Invaluable resource for fashion, costume historians. Approximately 725 illustrations. 128pp. 8⅜ x 11¼. 27276-1

THE 1912 AND 1915 GUSTAV STICKLEY FURNITURE CATALOGS, Gustav Stickley. With over 200 detailed illustrations and descriptions, these two catalogs are essential reading and reference materials and identification guides for Stickley furniture. Captions cite materials, dimensions and prices. 112pp. 6½ x 9¼. 26676-1

EARLY AMERICAN LOCOMOTIVES, John H. White, Jr. Finest locomotive engravings from early 19th century: historical (1804–74), main-line (after 1870), special, foreign, etc. 147 plates. 142pp. 11⅜ x 8¼. 22772-3

THE TALL SHIPS OF TODAY IN PHOTOGRAPHS, Frank O. Braynard. Lavishly illustrated tribute to nearly 100 majestic contemporary sailing vessels: Amerigo Vespucci, Clearwater, Constitution, Eagle, Mayflower, Sea Cloud, Victory, many more. Authoritative captions provide statistics, background on each ship. 190 black-and-white photographs and illustrations. Introduction. 128pp. 8⅞ x 11¾. 27163-3

LITTLE BOOK OF EARLY AMERICAN CRAFTS AND TRADES, Peter Stockham (ed.). 1807 children's book explains crafts and trades: baker, hatter, cooper, potter, and many others. 23 copperplate illustrations. 140pp. 4⅝ x 6. 23336-7

VICTORIAN FASHIONS AND COSTUMES FROM HARPER'S BAZAR, 1867–1898, Stella Blum (ed.). Day costumes, evening wear, sports clothes, shoes, hats, other accessories in over 1,000 detailed engravings. 320pp. 9⅜ x 12¼. 22990-4

GUSTAV STICKLEY, THE CRAFTSMAN, Mary Ann Smith. Superb study surveys broad scope of Stickley's achievement, especially in architecture. Design philosophy, rise and fall of the Craftsman empire, descriptions and floor plans for many Craftsman houses, more. 86 black-and-white halftones. 31 line illustrations. Introduction 208pp. 6½ x 9¼. 27210-9

THE LONG ISLAND RAIL ROAD IN EARLY PHOTOGRAPHS, Ron Ziel. Over 220 rare photos, informative text document origin (1844) and development of rail service on Long Island. Vintage views of early trains, locomotives, stations, passengers, crews, much more. Captions. 8⅞ x 11¾. 26301-0

VOYAGE OF THE LIBERDADE, Joshua Slocum. Great 19th-century mariner's thrilling, first-hand account of the wreck of his ship off South America, the 35-foot boat he built from the wreckage, and its remarkable voyage home. 128pp. 5⅜ x 8½. 40022-0

TEN BOOKS ON ARCHITECTURE, Vitruvius. The most important book ever written on architecture. Early Roman aesthetics, technology, classical orders, site selection, all other aspects. Morgan translation. 331pp. 5⅜ x 8½. 20645-9

THE HUMAN FIGURE IN MOTION, Eadweard Muybridge. More than 4,500 stopped-action photos, in action series, showing undraped men, women, children jumping, lying down, throwing, sitting, wrestling, carrying, etc. 390pp. 7⅞ x 10⅝. 20204-6 Clothbd.

TREES OF THE EASTERN AND CENTRAL UNITED STATES AND CANADA, William M. Harlow. Best one-volume guide to 140 trees. Full descriptions, woodlore, range, etc. Over 600 illustrations. Handy size. 288pp. 4½ x 6⅜. 20395-6

SONGS OF WESTERN BIRDS, Dr. Donald J. Borror. Complete song and call repertoire of 60 western species, including flycatchers, juncoes, cactus wrens, many more–includes fully illustrated booklet. Cassette and manual 99913-0

GROWING AND USING HERBS AND SPICES, Milo Miloradovich. Versatile handbook provides all the information needed for cultivation and use of all the herbs and spices available in North America. 4 illustrations. Index. Glossary. 236pp. 5⅜ x 8½. 25058-X

BIG BOOK OF MAZES AND LABYRINTHS, Walter Shepherd. 50 mazes and labyrinths in all–classical, solid, ripple, and more–in one great volume. Perfect inexpensive puzzler for clever youngsters. Full solutions. 112pp. 8⅛ x 11. 22951-3

PIANO TUNING, J. Cree Fischer. Clearest, best book for beginner, amateur. Simple repairs, raising dropped notes, tuning by easy method of flattened fifths. No previous skills needed. 4 illustrations. 201pp. 5⅜ x 8½.   23267-0

HINTS TO SINGERS, Lillian Nordica. Selecting the right teacher, developing confidence, overcoming stage fright, and many other important skills receive thoughtful discussion in this indispensible guide, written by a world-famous diva of four decades' experience. 96pp. 5⅜ x 8½.   40094-8

THE COMPLETE NONSENSE OF EDWARD LEAR, Edward Lear. All nonsense limericks, zany alphabets, Owl and Pussycat, songs, nonsense botany, etc., illustrated by Lear. Total of 320pp. 5⅜ x 8½. (Available in U.S. only.)   20167-8

VICTORIAN PARLOUR POETRY: An Annotated Anthology, Michael R. Turner. 117 gems by Longfellow, Tennyson, Browning, many lesser-known poets. "The Village Blacksmith," "Curfew Must Not Ring Tonight," "Only a Baby Small," dozens more, often difficult to find elsewhere. Index of poets, titles, first lines. xxiii + 325pp. 5⅜ x 8¼.   27044-0

DUBLINERS, James Joyce. Fifteen stories offer vivid, tightly focused observations of the lives of Dublin's poorer classes. At least one, "The Dead," is considered a masterpiece. Reprinted complete and unabridged from standard edition. 160pp. 5³⁄₁₆ x 8¼.   26870-5

GREAT WEIRD TALES: 14 Stories by Lovecraft, Blackwood, Machen and Others, S. T. Joshi (ed.). 14 spellbinding tales, including "The Sin Eater," by Fiona McLeod, "The Eye Above the Mantel," by Frank Belknap Long, as well as renowned works by R. H. Barlow, Lord Dunsany, Arthur Machen, W. C. Morrow and eight other masters of the genre. 256pp. 5⅜ x 8½. (Available in U.S. only.)   40436-6

THE BOOK OF THE SACRED MAGIC OF ABRAMELIN THE MAGE, translated by S. MacGregor Mathers. Medieval manuscript of ceremonial magic. Basic document in Aleister Crowley, Golden Dawn groups. 268pp. 5⅜ x 8½.   23211-5

NEW RUSSIAN-ENGLISH AND ENGLISH-RUSSIAN DICTIONARY, M. A. O'Brien. This is a remarkably handy Russian dictionary, containing a surprising amount of information, including over 70,000 entries. 366pp. 4½ x 6⅛.   20208-9

HISTORIC HOMES OF THE AMERICAN PRESIDENTS, Second, Revised Edition, Irvin Haas. A traveler's guide to American Presidential homes, most open to the public, depicting and describing homes occupied by every American President from George Washington to George Bush. With visiting hours, admission charges, travel routes. 175 photographs. Index. 160pp. 8¼ x 11.   26751-2

NEW YORK IN THE FORTIES, Andreas Feininger. 162 brilliant photographs by the well-known photographer, formerly with *Life* magazine. Commuters, shoppers, Times Square at night, much else from city at its peak. Captions by John von Hartz. 181pp. 9¼ x 10¾.   23585-8

INDIAN SIGN LANGUAGE, William Tomkins. Over 525 signs developed by Sioux and other tribes. Written instructions and diagrams. Also 290 pictographs. 111pp. 6⅛ x 9¼.   22029-X

ANATOMY: A Complete Guide for Artists, Joseph Sheppard. A master of figure drawing shows artists how to render human anatomy convincingly. Over 460 illustrations. 224pp. 8⅜ x 11¼. 27279-6

MEDIEVAL CALLIGRAPHY: Its History and Technique, Marc Drogin. Spirited history, comprehensive instruction manual covers 13 styles (ca. 4th century through 15th). Excellent photographs; directions for duplicating medieval techniques with modern tools. 224pp. 8⅜ x 11¼. 26142-5

DRIED FLOWERS: How to Prepare Them, Sarah Whitlock and Martha Rankin. Complete instructions on how to use silica gel, meal and borax, perlite aggregate, sand and borax, glycerine and water to create attractive permanent flower arrangements. 12 illustrations. 32pp. 5⅜ x 8½. 21802-3

EASY-TO-MAKE BIRD FEEDERS FOR WOODWORKERS, Scott D. Campbell. Detailed, simple-to-use guide for designing, constructing, caring for and using feeders. Text, illustrations for 12 classic and contemporary designs. 96pp. 5⅜ x 8½.

25847-5

SCOTTISH WONDER TALES FROM MYTH AND LEGEND, Donald A. Mackenzie. 16 lively tales tell of giants rumbling down mountainsides, of a magic wand that turns stone pillars into warriors, of gods and goddesses, evil hags, powerful forces and more. 240pp. 5⅜ x 8½. 29677-6

THE HISTORY OF UNDERCLOTHES, C. Willett Cunnington and Phyllis Cunnington. Fascinating, well-documented survey covering six centuries of English undergarments, enhanced with over 100 illustrations: 12th-century laced-up bodice, footed long drawers (1795), 19th-century bustles, l9th-century corsets for men, Victorian "bust improvers," much more. 272pp. 5⅜ x 8¼. 27124-2

ARTS AND CRAFTS FURNITURE: The Complete Brooks Catalog of 1912, Brooks Manufacturing Co. Photos and detailed descriptions of more than 150 now very collectible furniture designs from the Arts and Crafts movement depict davenports, settees, buffets, desks, tables, chairs, bedsteads, dressers and more, all built of solid, quarter-sawed oak. Invaluable for students and enthusiasts of antiques, Americana and the decorative arts. 80pp. 6½ x 9¼. 27471-3

WILBUR AND ORVILLE: A Biography of the Wright Brothers, Fred Howard. Definitive, crisply written study tells the full story of the brothers' lives and work. A vividly written biography, unparalleled in scope and color, that also captures the spirit of an extraordinary era. 560pp. 6⅛ x 9¼. 40297-5

THE ARTS OF THE SAILOR: Knotting, Splicing and Ropework, Hervey Garrett Smith. Indispensable shipboard reference covers tools, basic knots and useful hitches; handsewing and canvas work, more. Over 100 illustrations. Delightful reading for sea lovers. 256pp. 5⅜ x 8½. 26440-8

FRANK LLOYD WRIGHT'S FALLINGWATER: The House and Its History, Second, Revised Edition, Donald Hoffmann. A total revision–both in text and illustrations–of the standard document on Fallingwater, the boldest, most personal architectural statement of Wright's mature years, updated with valuable new material from the recently opened Frank Lloyd Wright Archives. "Fascinating"–*The New York Times*. 116 illustrations. 128pp. 9¼ x 10¾. 27430-6

PHOTOGRAPHIC SKETCHBOOK OF THE CIVIL WAR, Alexander Gardner. 100 photos taken on field during the Civil War. Famous shots of Manassas Harper's Ferry, Lincoln, Richmond, slave pens, etc. 244pp. 10⅝ x 8¼. 22731-6

FIVE ACRES AND INDEPENDENCE, Maurice G. Kains. Great back-to-the-land classic explains basics of self-sufficient farming. The one book to get. 95 illustrations. 397pp. 5⅜ x 8½. 20974-1

SONGS OF EASTERN BIRDS, Dr. Donald J. Borror. Songs and calls of 60 species most common to eastern U.S.: warblers, woodpeckers, flycatchers, thrushes, larks, many more in high-quality recording. Cassette and manual 99912-2

A MODERN HERBAL, Margaret Grieve. Much the fullest, most exact, most useful compilation of herbal material. Gigantic alphabetical encyclopedia, from aconite to zedoary, gives botanical information, medical properties, folklore, economic uses, much else. Indispensable to serious reader. 161 illustrations. 888pp. 6½ x 9¼. 2-vol. set. (Available in U.S. only.) Vol. I: 22798-7
Vol. II: 22799-5

HIDDEN TREASURE MAZE BOOK, Dave Phillips. Solve 34 challenging mazes accompanied by heroic tales of adventure. Evil dragons, people-eating plants, blood-thirsty giants, many more dangerous adversaries lurk at every twist and turn. 34 mazes, stories, solutions. 48pp. 8¼ x 11. 24566-7

LETTERS OF W. A. MOZART, Wolfgang A. Mozart. Remarkable letters show bawdy wit, humor, imagination, musical insights, contemporary musical world; includes some letters from Leopold Mozart. 276pp. 5⅜ x 8½. 22859-2

BASIC PRINCIPLES OF CLASSICAL BALLET, Agrippina Vaganova. Great Russian theoretician, teacher explains methods for teaching classical ballet. 118 illustrations. 175pp. 5⅜ x 8½. 22036-2

THE JUMPING FROG, Mark Twain. Revenge edition. The original story of The Celebrated Jumping Frog of Calaveras County, a hapless French translation, and Twain's hilarious "retranslation" from the French. 12 illustrations. 66pp. 5⅜ x 8½. 22686-7

BEST REMEMBERED POEMS, Martin Gardner (ed.). The 126 poems in this superb collection of 19th- and 20th-century British and American verse range from Shelley's "To a Skylark" to the impassioned "Renascence" of Edna St. Vincent Millay and to Edward Lear's whimsical "The Owl and the Pussycat." 224pp. 5⅜ x 8½. 27165-X

COMPLETE SONNETS, William Shakespeare. Over 150 exquisite poems deal with love, friendship, the tyranny of time, beauty's evanescence, death and other themes in language of remarkable power, precision and beauty. Glossary of archaic terms. 80pp. 5$\frac{3}{16}$ x 8¼. 26686-9

THE BATTLES THAT CHANGED HISTORY, Fletcher Pratt. Eminent historian profiles 16 crucial conflicts, ancient to modern, that changed the course of civilization. 352pp. 5⅜ x 8½. 41129-X

THE WIT AND HUMOR OF OSCAR WILDE, Alvin Redman (ed.). More than 1,000 ripostes, paradoxes, wisecracks: Work is the curse of the drinking classes; I can resist everything except temptation; etc. 258pp. 5⅜ x 8½.   20602-5

SHAKESPEARE LEXICON AND QUOTATION DICTIONARY, Alexander Schmidt. Full definitions, locations, shades of meaning in every word in plays and poems. More than 50,000 exact quotations. 1,485pp. 6½ x 9¼. 2-vol. set.
Vol. 1: 22726-X
Vol. 2: 22727-8

SELECTED POEMS, Emily Dickinson. Over 100 best-known, best-loved poems by one of America's foremost poets, reprinted from authoritative early editions. No comparable edition at this price. Index of first lines. 64pp. 5³⁄₁₆ x 8¼.   26466-1

THE INSIDIOUS DR. FU-MANCHU, Sax Rohmer. The first of the popular mystery series introduces a pair of English detectives to their archnemesis, the diabolical Dr. Fu-Manchu. Flavorful atmosphere, fast-paced action, and colorful characters enliven this classic of the genre. 208pp. 5³⁄₁₆ x 8¼.   29898-1

THE MALLEUS MALEFICARUM OF KRAMER AND SPRENGER, translated by Montague Summers. Full text of most important witchhunter's "bible," used by both Catholics and Protestants. 278pp. 6⅝ x 10.   22802-9

SPANISH STORIES/CUENTOS ESPAÑOLES: A Dual-Language Book, Angel Flores (ed.). Unique format offers 13 great stories in Spanish by Cervantes, Borges, others. Faithful English translations on facing pages. 352pp. 5⅜ x 8½.   25399-6

GARDEN CITY, LONG ISLAND, IN EARLY PHOTOGRAPHS, 1869–1919, Mildred H. Smith. Handsome treasury of 118 vintage pictures, accompanied by carefully researched captions, document the Garden City Hotel fire (1899), the Vanderbilt Cup Race (1908), the first airmail flight departing from the Nassau Boulevard Aerodrome (1911), and much more. 96pp. 8⅞ x 11¾.   40669-5

OLD QUEENS, N.Y., IN EARLY PHOTOGRAPHS, Vincent F. Seyfried and William Asadorian. Over 160 rare photographs of Maspeth, Jamaica, Jackson Heights, and other areas. Vintage views of DeWitt Clinton mansion, 1939 World's Fair and more. Captions. 192pp. 8⅞ x 11.   26358-4

CAPTURED BY THE INDIANS: 15 Firsthand Accounts, 1750-1870, Frederick Drimmer. Astounding true historical accounts of grisly torture, bloody conflicts, relentless pursuits, miraculous escapes and more, by people who lived to tell the tale. 384pp. 5⅜ x 8½.   24901-8

THE WORLD'S GREAT SPEECHES (Fourth Enlarged Edition), Lewis Copeland, Lawrence W. Lamm, and Stephen J. McKenna. Nearly 300 speeches provide public speakers with a wealth of updated quotes and inspiration–from Pericles' funeral oration and William Jennings Bryan's "Cross of Gold Speech" to Malcolm X's powerful words on the Black Revolution and Earl of Spenser's tribute to his sister, Diana, Princess of Wales. 944pp. 5⅜ x 8⅜.   40903-1

THE BOOK OF THE SWORD, Sir Richard F. Burton. Great Victorian scholar/adventurer's eloquent, erudite history of the "queen of weapons"–from prehistory to early Roman Empire. Evolution and development of early swords, variations (sabre, broadsword, cutlass, scimitar, etc.), much more. 336pp. 6⅛ x 9¼.
25434-8

AUTOBIOGRAPHY: The Story of My Experiments with Truth, Mohandas K. Gandhi. Boyhood, legal studies, purification, the growth of the Satyagraha (nonviolent protest) movement. Critical, inspiring work of the man responsible for the freedom of India. 480pp. 5⅜ x 8½. (Available in U.S. only.)   24593-4

CELTIC MYTHS AND LEGENDS, T. W. Rolleston. Masterful retelling of Irish and Welsh stories and tales. Cuchulain, King Arthur, Deirdre, the Grail, many more. First paperback edition. 58 full-page illustrations. 512pp. 5⅜ x 8½.   26507-2

THE PRINCIPLES OF PSYCHOLOGY, William James. Famous long course complete, unabridged. Stream of thought, time perception, memory, experimental methods; great work decades ahead of its time. 94 figures. 1,391pp. 5⅜ x 8½. 2-vol. set.
Vol. I: 20381-6   Vol. II: 20382-4

THE WORLD AS WILL AND REPRESENTATION, Arthur Schopenhauer. Definitive English translation of Schopenhauer's life work, correcting more than 1,000 errors, omissions in earlier translations. Translated by E. F. J. Payne. Total of 1,269pp. 5⅜ x 8½. 2-vol. set.   Vol. 1: 21761-2   Vol. 2: 21762-0

MAGIC AND MYSTERY IN TIBET, Madame Alexandra David-Neel. Experiences among lamas, magicians, sages, sorcerers, Bonpa wizards. A true psychic discovery. 32 illustrations. 321pp. 5⅜ x 8½. (Available in U.S. only.)   22682-4

THE EGYPTIAN BOOK OF THE DEAD, E. A. Wallis Budge. Complete reproduction of Ani's papyrus, finest ever found. Full hieroglyphic text, interlinear transliteration, word-for-word translation, smooth translation. 533pp. 6½ x 9¼.   21866-X

MATHEMATICS FOR THE NONMATHEMATICIAN, Morris Kline. Detailed, college-level treatment of mathematics in cultural and historical context, with numerous exercises. Recommended Reading Lists. Tables. Numerous figures. 641pp. 5⅜ x 8½.
24823-2

PROBABILISTIC METHODS IN THE THEORY OF STRUCTURES, Isaac Elishakoff. Well-written introduction covers the elements of the theory of probability from two or more random variables, the reliability of such multivariable structures, the theory of random function, Monte Carlo methods of treating problems incapable of exact solution, and more. Examples. 502pp. 5⅜ x 8½.   40691-1

THE RIME OF THE ANCIENT MARINER, Gustave Doré, S. T. Coleridge. Doré's finest work; 34 plates capture moods, subtleties of poem. Flawless full-size reproductions printed on facing pages with authoritative text of poem. "Beautiful. Simply beautiful."–*Publisher's Weekly.* 77pp. 9¼ x 12.   22305-1

NORTH AMERICAN INDIAN DESIGNS FOR ARTISTS AND CRAFTSPEOPLE, Eva Wilson. Over 360 authentic copyright-free designs adapted from Navajo blankets, Hopi pottery, Sioux buffalo hides, more. Geometrics, symbolic figures, plant and animal motifs, etc. 128pp. 8⅜ x 11. (Not for sale in the United Kingdom.)   25341-4

SCULPTURE: Principles and Practice, Louis Slobodkin. Step-by-step approach to clay, plaster, metals, stone; classical and modern. 253 drawings, photos. 255pp. 8⅛ x 11.
22960-2

THE INFLUENCE OF SEA POWER UPON HISTORY, 1660–1783, A. T. Mahan. Influential classic of naval history and tactics still used as text in war colleges. First paperback edition. 4 maps. 24 battle plans. 640pp. 5⅜ x 8½.   25509-3

CATALOG OF DOVER BOOKS

THE STORY OF THE TITANIC AS TOLD BY ITS SURVIVORS, Jack Winocour (ed.). What it was really like. Panic, despair, shocking inefficiency, and a little heroism. More thrilling than any fictional account. 26 illustrations. 320pp. 5⅜ x 8½.
20610-6

FAIRY AND FOLK TALES OF THE IRISH PEASANTRY, William Butler Yeats (ed.). Treasury of 64 tales from the twilight world of Celtic myth and legend: "The Soul Cages," "The Kildare Pooka," "King O'Toole and his Goose," many more. Introduction and Notes by W. B. Yeats. 352pp. 5⅜ x 8½.
26941-8

BUDDHIST MAHAYANA TEXTS, E. B. Cowell and others (eds.). Superb, accurate translations of basic documents in Mahayana Buddhism, highly important in history of religions. The Buddha-karita of Asvaghosha, Larger Sukhavativyuha, more. 448pp. 5⅜ x 8½.
25552-2

ONE TWO THREE . . . INFINITY: Facts and Speculations of Science, George Gamow. Great physicist's fascinating, readable overview of contemporary science: number theory, relativity, fourth dimension, entropy, genes, atomic structure, much more. 128 illustrations. Index. 352pp. 5⅜ x 8½.
25664-2

EXPERIMENTATION AND MEASUREMENT, W. J. Youden. Introductory manual explains laws of measurement in simple terms and offers tips for achieving accuracy and minimizing errors. Mathematics of measurement, use of instruments, experimenting with machines. 1994 edition. Foreword. Preface. Introduction. Epilogue. Selected Readings. Glossary. Index. Tables and figures. 128pp. 5⅜ x 8½. 40451-X

DALÍ ON MODERN ART: The Cuckolds of Antiquated Modern Art, Salvador Dalí. Influential painter skewers modern art and its practitioners. Outrageous evaluations of Picasso, Cézanne, Turner, more. 15 renderings of paintings discussed. 44 calligraphic decorations by Dalí. 96pp. 5⅜ x 8½. (Available in U.S. only.)
29220-7

ANTIQUE PLAYING CARDS: A Pictorial History, Henry René D'Allemagne. Over 900 elaborate, decorative images from rare playing cards (14th–20th centuries): Bacchus, death, dancing dogs, hunting scenes, royal coats of arms, players cheating, much more. 96pp. 9¼ x 12¼.
29265-7

MAKING FURNITURE MASTERPIECES: 30 Projects with Measured Drawings, Franklin H. Gottshall. Step-by-step instructions, illustrations for constructing handsome, useful pieces, among them a Sheraton desk, Chippendale chair, Spanish desk, Queen Anne table and a William and Mary dressing mirror. 224pp. 8⅛ x 11¼.
29338-6

THE FOSSIL BOOK: A Record of Prehistoric Life, Patricia V. Rich et al. Profusely illustrated definitive guide covers everything from single-celled organisms and dinosaurs to birds and mammals and the interplay between climate and man. Over 1,500 illustrations. 760pp. 7½ x 10⅛.
29371-8

Paperbound unless otherwise indicated. Available at your book dealer, online at **www.doverpublications.com**, or by writing to Dept. GI, Dover Publications, Inc., 31 East 2nd Street, Mineola, NY 11501. For current price information or for free catalogues (please indicate field of interest), write to Dover Publications or log on to **www.doverpublications.com** and see every Dover book in print. Dover publishes more than 500 books each year on science, elementary and advanced mathematics, biology, music, art, literary history, social sciences, and other areas.